HUMANISTIC ETHICS

Humanistic Ethics

by GARDNER WILLIAMS

Professor of Philosophy
University of Toledo

PHILOSOPHICAL LIBRARY
NEW YORK

PREFACE

IN this book I am proposing three seeming paradoxes, which, I shall maintain, do not in fact involve any contradictions. These are (1) ultimate ethics is purely individualistic, but social obligations and the universal categorical imperative are valid. (2) Man's free-will is based upon an absolute causal determinism. (3) The true essence of religion fits perfectly into a metaphysics of emergent evolutionary naturalism which ignores or denies supernaturalism and cosmic teleology.

Chapter 1 partly summarizes the rest of the book and contrasts its principles of *hedonic individual relativism* with popular thought on ethics.

Chapter 2 gives the cultural and scientific background, and the sources of hedonic individual relativism.

Chapters 3, 4, and 5 give the essentials of the value theory.

Chapter 3 is the ultimate individualistic theory.

Chapter 4 deduces social obligation from this.

Chapter 5 elucidates the three senses in which ethics are universal.

Chapters 6, 7, and 8 supply the indispensable foundation in psychological descriptions upon which all the abstract theory of chapters 3, 4, and 5 rests.

Chapters 6 and 7 describe the major interests or desires

whose persistent motivation in large measure constitutes or generates man's moral experience. Chapter 8 describes the unity of the personality, and the retrospective, consummatory, and anticipatory aspects of the major interests, which bind most of the experiences of one biological organism into a unified self or personality with a considerable degree of continuity through time. This self is one of the most significant entities in the theory of moral obligation. All duty, and all good and evil, are either contained in such a self or else are relative to it.

Chapter 9 on *time* shows the cosmic status of value.

Chapters 10 and 11 analyze two traditional schools of thought, egoistic hedonism and utilitarianism, with which hedonic individual relativism is most closely connected and from which it is derived.

Chapters 12, 13, and 14 explain the nature of human freedom and of moral responsibility. Chapter 12 is the basic theory of freedom. Chapter 13 deals with some prevalent misunderstandings of it. Chapter 14 takes up the special problem of moral responsibility.

Chapter 15 shows how hedonic individual relativism applies to the fine arts and how its truth may be derived from a study of these.

Chapter 16 analyses religion systematically in the light of the principles already established.

The first seeming paradox, of individual vs. social and universal ethics, is found in chapters 3, 4, and 5. The second, of free-will vs. determinism, is considered in chapters 12, 13, and 14. The third, of true evolutionary naturalism vs. true religion, appears in chapter 2, sect. 2, 3, and in chapter 16.

ACKNOWLEDGMENTS

Many people have helped me write this book, chiefly by discussing the ideas in it with me. I am deeply indebted to hundreds of my former students at the University of Michigan, the University of Wisconsin, and the University of Toledo. Also I owe a great debt of gratitude to my teacher, the late DeWitt H. Parker, of the University of Michigan, for some of the basic ideas which I have expressed. I owe much to my friend, Morrison R. Van Cleve, for his patience and interest in helping me to express myself more clearly, and to my former student, Marjorie Goetze, for her criticisms and her help in preparing manuscript. I owe a very special debt to my colleague, Professor Hazel E. Barnes, for the final, indispensable, and drastic revision of the entire manuscript. And finally, and above all, I am indebted to my wife, without whose constant help in innumerable ways I could never have written this book.

Permission has been kindly granted by the *Journal of Philosophy* to reprint certain copyrighted material, in chapters 3, 4, 5, 12, and 14, which appeared in its issues of August 13, 1942, March 29, 1945, and November 18, 1948, and by the American Humanist Association to reprint copyrighted material, in chapter 12, from the *Humanist* for January 1949.

TABLE OF CONTENTS

xi

HUMANISTIC ETHICS

CHAPTER I

Humanism vs. Traditional Ethical Theory

ETHICS is the same thing as axiology or the general theory of value. It is an analysis of man's moral experience; that is, the experience of worth or value, of good and evil, of right and wrong, of duty and of beauty. A true ethics is a naturalistic ethics, and for man it is a humanistic ethics. All human ethical obligation grows out of human nature and out of man's natural experience.

Humanistic ethics will be found to contrast with traditional theories about the essential nature of value and duty in a number of ways, and will be best understood at the start by a study of some of these contrasts. Five of its principles are so sharply at variance with customary beliefs as perhaps to seem unethical to traditionally minded people. Nevertheless, as our discussion progresses, I think that the truth of these principles will become evident. The five are as follows:-

(1) All conscious life is in one sense absolutely selfish.

(2) The basic teaching of egoistic hedonism is true.

(3) Individual ethical relativism is true.

(4) The will to power is often good.

(5) It is sometimes one's duty to do what is evil to other people.

Let us examine each of these.

(1) The whole of man's conscious aim in life is abso-

3

lutely selfish in the rather unusual sense that it is his self, or is an expression of his self. Every interest and desire which a man experiences, even his love or benevolence toward other people, is a part of his self, and the satisfaction of it is his self-satisfaction. Its expression is his self-expression. This is no denial that love is purely unselfish in the ordinary sense of aiming at the welfare of another person as a final objective. Obviously such self-expression is not necessarily unethical.

(2) Egoistic hedonism, the teaching of Epicurus, about 300 B.C. in Athens, is true in so far as it asserts that individual feelings of satisfaction or pleasure are intrinsic value. Men do not use the terms *good* and *duty* properly unless they mean that some individual is being satisfied, or more satisfied or less dissatisfied, by what is good and by what is morally obligatory. Satisfaction or dissatisfaction are essential to the definition of these two terms.

It must of course be understood that sensory tickles, tingles, thrills, sweet tastes, and charming smells are different from the feeling of satisfaction. Also sensory pain is different from the feeling of dissatisfaction. I shall use the words satisfaction and dissatisfaction to mean feeling-tones, which are caused by physiological processes in the central nervous system and are not produced by any specific sensory end-organ. On the other hand, tickles and sweet tastes and smells and sensory pain are caused by sense organs. Sometimes a sensory pain can satisfy, as in masochism. So far as it does it is good. Sometimes a tickle or a sweet taste will dissatisfy. So far as it does it is bad.

Some other principles of Epicurus's teaching are false, such as the notions that men should or must always pursue their own feelings of pleasure or satisfaction as final objectives, and that man's highest good or value, the maximum of pleasure or satisfaction, will always be realized by taking the easy method of running away from major social problems and conflicts.

(3) Good and evil and duty are relative to individual points of view. This is individual ethical relativism, or subjectivism. The phrase 'individual relativism' has three meanings, two of which are false, but the third of which is a corner stone of sound ethics and value theory. The first false meaning is that 'there is nothing either good or bad but thinking makes it so.' This is the notion that one's opinion about anything determines its value. Value is regarded as relative to the cognition of it, to the imputation of it, or to what may be called 'valuation.' This view is confusedly expressed by William James in his book *The Will to Believe* (Longmans Green, 1898, pp. 190-193). The second false form of ethical relativism is the principle that one's feeling-attitudes of approval or disapproval toward a thing determine its value. James asserted this principle also (*loc. cit.*). So did Hume in his *Enquiry Concerning Morals* (Oxford Press, 1902, p. 289). And W. M. Urban says this in his *Valuation, Its Nature and Laws* (Geo. Allen and Unwin, London, 1909, p. 40). If one feels approval of a thing, it is supposed that that makes it good. If one feels disapproval, it is supposed that that makes it bad.

The error of both these theories should be obvious. Even though one thinks that an act is good or best and feels approval of it, it still may turn out to be disastrous and therefore bad. But a third form of ethical relativism is true. This is the principle that an act is best, and is morally obligatory, from the point of view of any individual, if it involves a maximum of satisfaction in the long run for that individual. To involve satisfaction means to contain it or to cause it. One's opinion about its value might affect one's feeling toward it, and one's feeling-attitudes of approval or disapproval would be involved in its value, but would not usually be the only feeling involved. All other feelings in the individual's life contained in the experience of the act, or resulting from it, would also be determining factors in its value for that individual.

(4) Selfish ambition, or the will to power, when successful, is intrinsically good because it is intrinsically satisfactory. Moreover, in certain forms and degrees, when guided by reason, it is an indispensable part of a good life. An individual who never enjoyed exercising influence or power over others for his own good would be abnormal and could not measure up socially.

(5) Sometimes an individual has a duty to do what is an evil to other persons. Duties are relative to individual points of view, and there are times when these clash. What is best for one may be evil for others. If democratic countries fight to defend their humane institutions against dictatorships, it may be best for a democratic citizen-soldier to kill some of the soldiers of the dictator. The armed forces of the United States of America killed a lot of 'dictatorial' soldiers, as well as civilians, between December 1941 and August 1945. Being killed may have been an evil to those soldiers and civilians from their own points of view. In losing their lives they may have lost what would have been worth while to them in the long run. At least it might have been better than nothing.

I have derived the five truths listed here from experience interpreted by reason, with the aid of certain particularly helpful elements in the tradition of Western Civilization.

I shall try to explain the importance of these traditional and cultural elements in chapter 2. Their significance for our inquiry is very great. Without them our understanding of the principles of ethics could not have been carried beyond the primitive level of the dominant traditional thought of our age. It must be borne in mind that these particularly helpful traditions are mostly subordinate cultural factors in contemporary society, and are not highly regarded by the powerful persons who direct the thinking of the great masses of the people, and thus not by the masses of the people themselves. The popular and dominant tradition of our western society has missed all five truths, and tends to condemn them whenever it is aware of them. There are three reasons why it does so and why it is so far removed from the truth about some other aspects of ethics. (1) The subject is difficult and the human mind is limited in its capacity. The people who created our ethical tradition, and those who now maintain it, have made some mistakes because they were or are not fully able to understand the subject. (2) Their aberrations are also due in part to a combination of the two facts, that they have properly taken with deadly earnestness the business of upholding the good in human society and that this good apparently could not be upheld without some inaccuracy of statement. Falsehood has been, or has seemed, necessary because the bulk of the people involved were ignorant and primitive in their thinking. False ethical theory has often been more efficacious than true theory in making the behavior of simple folk ethical. The subjects of an Egyptian Pharoah were more influenced to cooperate with his government by being told that he was descended from the sun god, than they would have been if their spiritual preceptors had merely pointed out the advantages to them, and to those whom they loved, of the protection and order which his rule afforded. If you tell such people the truth about why they should do their duty, they will do something else. Many customary rules of conduct and customary reasons given for following them, have been instigated by intelligent leaders in church and state primarily for the purpose of making society a wholesome and successful joint enterprise. In order to attain this objective they have had to ignore considerations of truthfulness because of the kind of people with whom they were dealing. (3) These leaders have also unquestionably been motivated in part by a perfectly understandable desire to have their own church or state supervise the practice of the basic virtues. In part, traditional ethical teaching has been selfish institutional propaganda in which truthfulness was a minor consideration if it was considered at all.

Besides denying the five truths which I have stated, our dominant ethical tradition has sponsored important errors which we may list under eight headings as follows: It has taught

(1) that ethics is impossible without cosmic teleology or supernaturalism;

(2) that the rewards and punishments of an after life are indispensable for a good life now;

(3) that the belief in these is also indispensable;

(4) that human nature is essentially depraved, due to original sin, and consequently that man is utterly incapable of finding salvation (or self-respect or happiness) by natural means;

(5) that puritanism and asceticism are the highest morality;

(6) that brotherly love is the only ultimate ethical imperative;

(7) that purity of heart is essential to the degree that a mere desire to do evil, not acted on, is just as bad as acting on it.

Moreover this traditional theory has discouraged serious rational enquiry into the real nature of the good by giving to many the impression

(8) that the only way ethics can be profitably discussed is in the manner of preaching; that is, of urging people with some emotional fervor to live up to a moral standard. Popularly, that is about the only way ethics is treated. As a result many persons fail to realize that anything significant can be said on the subject which is not exhortation. Some even resent the existence of an ethical discourse which is not a sermon.

All of these intellectual aberrations have had practical value as instruments of social control. They have helped make human society orderly and prosperous. They have thus in some ways raised the level of civilization and of human happiness. But they have been impediments to genuine understanding. In our present study we shall aim chiefly at understanding. This should prove worth while for those who wish to understand. Also it will probably be a help to some in living a good life.

Our theory will be a naturalistic doctrine of self-reliance, self-realization, self-satisfaction, and self-assertion. To many persons it may seem strange that moral obligation can be firmly based upon a foundation so pervaded with selfishness. Nevertheless it can; and in fact it is. All moral obligations are derived from individual selves. Self-assertion involves love, prudent helpfulness, social cooperation, the

9

obligation and effort to maintain beneficent social institutions, and the obligation and effort to reform defective ones. The whole motivation and obligation for social and cultural progress is an expression of individual human nature, as stimulated, of course, by environmental factors, the most important of which often are other individuals organized into social institutions.

Moreover, an accurate analysis of the basic individualistic ethical principles reveals a categorical imperative and three valid kinds of universality, to be discussed more fully in chapters 3 and 5. These three universalities are (1) the absolutely universal validity of the principle of ethical relativism, (2) the universality of the obligation imposed upon all persons and things, from any one individual's point of view, to serve that individual's need, and (3) the universality of the truth about any particular good or duty.

CHAPTER II

The Cultural and Scientific Background of Humanistic Ethics

L ET us consider some of the cultural trends in Western Civilization which have been favorable to true insight in ethics. These will in some measure explain how humanistic ethics comes to exist and to be what it is.

One trend or strain in our culture is Tomistic theology. In the thirteenth century St. Thomas Aquinas adopted certain of the ethical truths taught by Aristotle, and made them part of our religious tradition. Aristotle (about 335 B.C. in Athens) was a very intelligent, civilized, and responsible person who studied ethical problems seriously in a stimulating, free, and secular society. Many of his ideas are true and important. One of these that Thomas borrowed is that God is man's highest good. God is the spirit or principle of the highest good. This really involves the further principle, not explicitly stated either by Aristotle or by the Saint, that the only real atheism is the denial of the spiritual validity of this ideal good. Thomas also said that the good is the object of desire, which is not quite true, but is a close and valuable approximation to the real truth that the good is the satisfactory. The satisfactory usually is so because it satisfies desire. Thomas also indicated truly that man's ultimate duty is the maximum of self-realization or the actualization of the essential self. Any

11

ethicist who discards these principles condemns himself before the tribunal of reason, experience, and truth.

But it can hardly be doubted that there have been real advantages in the deliverance of many in modern times from the strict ecclesiastical authoritarianism with which St. Thomas's Aristotelianism was linked. There has been a growing secularization in western culture ever since the end of the Middle Ages. The control of many human activities, such as education, has largely been transferred from churchmen to laymen. This has freed many minds from spiritual tyrannies which once blocked scientific truth, and which still block it in certain quarters. Contemporary culture is somewhat like that of the sixth and fifth centuries B.C. (600 B.C.-400 B.C.) in Greece, from which Aristotle (though he lived in the less flourishing fourth century) derived his inspiration. I think that in spite of undeniably grave perils, our age holds the promise of a creativity equal to that of the earlier Hellenic era.

The need for escaping from spiritual tyrannies is interpreted by some to mean that modern educated and enlightened man must repudiate religion. This is not true. Civilization has always depended upon the presence in men's hearts and minds of the true essence of religion, which is an active devotion to the ideal of man's highest good. This is the love of God. God is the ideal. Whether the notion of God as a force is true or not, it is spiritually and religiously superfluous. The preservation of civilization still depends upon the love of God. This can be expressed on a purely naturalistic basis without a trace of supernaturalism, cosmic teleology, superstition, or childish primitivism,—and in some quarters it is now being so expressed (see chapter 16).

In addition to Tomism and secularism, there are other important strains in western culture which are helpful to an understanding of the true principles of man's moral experience. Among these are the Aristotelian and Utilitarian traditions which recognize human happiness as the key concept in ethics. Also there is the Epicurean tradition of egoistic hedonism, mentioned in chapter 1, which teaches that happiness is essentially individual and hedonic. Hedonic means involving pleasure or the feeling of satisfaction.

Another important area of contemporary culture is aesthetics. In his *Analysis of Art,* chapter 2 (Yale University Press, 1926) and in his *Human Values,* chapters 4 and 15 (Geo. Wahr, Ann Arbor) Professor D. H. Parker has shown that art and morals are all part of the general field of values, and that most of the principles of fine art apply to the rest of life. Morals are used in far too narrow a sense if they are restricted to 'good' deeds of social helpfulness. In order to understand the true significance of helpfulness we must study the principles of all value, which are also exemplified in beauty, sensory pleasure, knowledge, self-assertion, glory, economic gain, and other value experiences. The meanings 'morality' and 'ethics' should cover the whole of axiology or general theory of value. As such, ethics includes aesthetics. Ethics deals with the good and with imperatives created by the good. Beauty is a kind of good because it satisfies. Things ought to be beautiful because beauty satisfies. Beauty creates imperatives which, according to the degree of their satisfactoriness, are truly moral imperatives.

Moreover, a number of very important principles, valid in aesthetics, will be found also to be valid throughout the value field. One of these, we have said, is hedonism. An-

13

other is individual relativity; and another is the principle of formal correctness or organic unity with its six subdivisions (see chapter 15).

Many principles from the tradition of modern science are important for the understanding of ethics. This will be disputed by some. It will be said that science describes what is or exists, while ethics deals with what ought to be. *What is* is often very different from *what ought to be*. This is true, but what ought to be is determined by certain things which are. The highest good or duty, for anyone, is, as we pointed out in chapter 1, that which is most deeply satisfactory to him in the long run. But what is satisfactory to one depends upon his actual nature. What is best for a canary bird is determined by the nature of the canary bird, and what is best for a man is determined by the nature of the man. Man's nature is a proper object of scientific inquiry, and is today in part known scientifically, chiefly by the sciences of biology, psychology, and sociology.

Also, theories about what ought to be can be perverted by factual errors in non-ethical fields. Let us consider some scientific truths which are especially significant as guides and warnings to the questing ethicist.

(1) There is the general principle of all science,—the uniformity of nature, also called determinism. This principle still stands, in spite of Heisenberg and Eddington. When properly understood it is perfectly consistent with free-will and moral responsibility (see chapters 12-14).

(2) There is the basic principle of the origin of human nature through the processes of biological evolution, which has occurred by means of the natural selection of chance variations and mutations. Man's background is among the lower animals and he still has important animal elements

14

in his nature. A fundamental naturalistic principle is that all emergent spiritual qualities have a biological basis. Humanistic ethics will usually and properly be associated with the metaphysics of emergent evolutionary naturalism, and with the denial of the container theory of causation, which theory holds that causes must have contained all of their effects (see chapter 10; ch. 13, sect. 3).

(3) From sociology and anthropology comes the concept of cultural (sometimes called social) evolution, which is the accumulation from generation to generation of invented and otherwise learned traits, transmitted by imitation and education, usually from older to younger individuals. This evolution accounts for man's living in a manner markedly different in some ways from that of the lower animals. Cultural evolution, by invention, discovery, imitation, and consequent accumulation, has produced in the human species a cultural heritage which now enables most men to live in a civilized manner. If a human organism grew up without receiving this heritage by imitation or education it would have no language, clothing, housing, urban life, agriculture, government, or industry, and its behavior would hardly be distinguishable from that of the lower animals, in spite of its innate abilities far in excess of any other species. Superior natural intelligence by itself is not a sufficient condition for the institutional life of civilized humanity or for the spiritual development of individual men. To their biological inheritance must be added the cultural inheritance, actually a product of a million years of cultural evolution, involving many techniques, rational insights, social institutions, and discipline, and providing the inspiration of stimulating social contacts.

Related to this cultural development, which has occurred

through the last million years of the Pleistocene period (the latest Ice Age) and the recent post-glacial era, is the biological evolution of man during that epoch, from the proto-man or pre-man of Pliocene (the geological age before Pleistocene), through the type of Sino-anthropos Pekingensis and Pithecanthropus Erectus, to the *homo sapiens* of the last 30,000 years or so. All contemporary men are *homo sapiens*. This improvement through Pleistocene in man's biologically inherited nature, by making men intellectually more capable, helped to further the cultural evolution that was going on at the same time.

It is important to realize that all cultural evolution is absolutely dependent upon biological evolution. Only those organisms with the human biological heredity have been able, through a million years or so of earthly experience under social and other environmental stimuli, to develop civilized life. It is also significant that the greatest cultural evolution has taken place in the last fifteen thousand years, and only after biological evolution put man at his present biologically inherited level of mental ability,—that of *homo sapiens*. In 20,000 B.C. man was a cave dwelling hunter who did not know enough to build houses or practice agriculture, though the innate ability of the various individuals probably was, on an average, equal to ours today. Since then the greatest advances have occurred and civilization has emerged.

The origin and development of man's body and spirit in the two evolutions, biological and cultural, should never be lost sight of in any theoretical inquiry into ethics.

Related to these evolutions is the sociological principle that society creates individuals. Their parents start them off, and then their souls develop both through biological maturation and through social contacts with parents and with other people. The acquired or non-innate aspects of every soul or personality are 99% or more copied from other people.

Finally, the social and cultural relativism of value must be recognized. Varying mores make some things right in certain societies which are wrong in other societies.

(4) There are a number of fundamentals from psychology.

All consciousness depends directly upon the nervous system and is an emergent property of the same. Also all free choice is determined by character, which is determined by heredity and environment, which is determined by ultimate reality, the substantial core of nature, absolute being, or the supreme being,—'being' here meaning just ultimate or basic existence, which might or might not be living, conscious, or personal.

Within the field of psychology also is included the study of human desire which is one of the most important factors in determining moral obligation. Obligation is ultimately a matter of the feeling of satisfaction, and most satisfaction is caused by the gratification or fulfillment of desire. There are certain basic and persistent desires or major interests in the heart of man which constitute the chief experiential content of the self, soul, or personality, which are the chief motivations in life, and whose maximum gratification is the highest good. These are love, ambition, self-preservation, sensory pleasure, knowledge, play, beauty, efficiency, and harmony (see chapters 6-7).

The dynamic psychology of Freud and Jung and others has taught us that some of the most important aspects of desire are subconscious. In order to live happily we should know as much about the subconscious as possible. The

17

recent studies by Karl Menninger (*Man Against Himself*, Harcourt Brace), Erich Fromm (*Man For Himself*, Rinehart & Co.), Karen Horney (*The Neurotic Personality of Our Time*, W. W. Norton), and Joshua L. Liebman (*Peace of Mind*, Simon & Schuster), are of great importance for the understanding of humanistic ethics.

(5) Modern physics suggests the important principle that the ultimate reality or metaphysical absolute or supreme being is structured energy, which has always existed, and will always exist. Everything that happens is probably a form of this energy. Whether it functions purposively and consciously, or not, cannot be proved or disproved.

This supreme being is not God. God, as we pointed out earlier, is the ideal of man's highest good. God and the supreme being must be distinguished. God should be loved, and we may be piously grateful, if we feel so inclined, to the supreme being for all of our blessings (see chapter 16).

(6) The method of inquiry into ethics in this book is an important part of the traditional method of science. It is a combination of empiricism and rationalism. We may call it *empirical rationalism*. Always, in the quest for any knowledge, man should use reason to interpret experience. That is the most likely way to discover the truth.

My empiricism is methodological and epistemological, not metaphysical. I do not assert, what Hume and Comte appear to have thought some of the time, that experience is all that exists. I think that probably an intrinsically non-experiential substance lurks behind surface experience. One should not dogmatize too confidently about this, but the uniformity of nature indicates to me that there is some kind of a *ding an sich* back there keeping causation uniform.

18

And, as I said, modern physics suggests that it is structured energy.

Also the rationalism herein is epistemological and not metaphysical. It does not assert that the substance of things is rational or is reason itself. Nor does it say that the universe as a whole operates in accordance with reason. It merely maintains that man ought to be as rational as possible in his beliefs. In doing so he will be exercising his *theoretical* reason. Incidentally he ought also to be as rational as possible in his actions. In doing so he will be exercising his *practical* reason; that is, he will be adapting means efficiently to the attainment of good ends. The ethics of this book is, in this sense, an axiological rationalism,—which however will in no way minimize the axiological primacy of desire and feeling.

Reason is partly the interpretation of empirical evidence. Probability is the strength or probative efficacy of this evidence as so interpreted. Belief should be based on high probabilities. It would be still better to have it based on certainties, but we cannot have strict rational certainty in anything important.[1] Probability leads to the belief in such scientific truths as we have mentioned in this chapter.

Another aspect of reason is Socratic dialectic. This is one of the basic methodological principles which must be used in any cognitive inquiry, and specifically in the present inquiry into the principles of ethics. I do not mean that from now on I shall throw the discussion into the form of a dialogue. The real essence of Socratic dialectic is to employ strict definitions, develop their implications rationally, and hold only to those in which all of the implications are ac-

---

[1] See my paper "Absolute Truth and the Shadow of Doubt" in *Philosophy of Science*, July 1948, Vol. 15, No. 3.

ceptable in the light of other definitions and of experience. Every definition, together with its implications, must be consistent with every other definition and its implications. Dialectic is deductive logic. It is defining one's terms the way one is going to use them and then using them the way one has defined them. It is finding the right definition, which will enable one to deal with the subject understandably, and then using that definition consistently. Correct dialectic gives clarity of thought. This is no guarantee of truth, Plato and Descartes to the contrary notwithstanding; but without the clarity which dialectic alone can give, the truth cannot be discovered.

The definitions must not be arbitrary. Though dialectic is essentially a rational process, it is not independent of experience. All definitions and all implications must be tested empirically for their agreement with experience as well as rationally for their logical coherence. They should grow out of experience. They must give an understanding of it. The definitions which I shall offer in chapter 3 are the only ones with which I am familiar in the field of ethics which seem to me capable of surviving both the empirical and the dialectical-logical tests.

Dialectic is an essential part of any cognitive inquiry. Without consistently held definitions no thought can rise to the status of knowledge. Unfortunately dialectic is now flouted in some pragmatic-scientific circles. Its importance was first clearly recognized in ancient Greece in the fifth century B. C. Its nature is revealed in the following quotation from Plato's *Republic* (about 387 B.C.) section 534. "Socrates— 'Until a person is able to abstract and define rationally the idea of the good, and unless he can run the gauntlet of all objections, and is ready to disprove them, not by appeals to opinion, but to absolute truth, never faltering at any step in the argument— unless he can do all this, you would say he knows neither the idea of the good nor any other good; he apprehends only a shadow if anything at all, which is given by opinion and not by science;— dreaming and slumbering in this life, before he is well awake here, he arrives at the world below, and has his final quietus.' " (Jowett trans., 3rd ed., Oxford Press). There is some exaggeration here, but it is the exaggeration of an important truth.

Let us define the good and the best, and let us run our definitions through the gauntlet of all possible objections, disproving every objection, if we can, by reason and experience.

CHAPTER III

Hedonic Individual Relativism

I SHALL define and recommend an ethical or axiological terminology which has seemed to me adequate for the expression of all the valid principles of man's moral experience. I shall try to show, by the use of this terminology, that (1) there is a sense in which ethics is purely individualistic, (2) there is another sense in which it is social, and (3) there are three other senses in which it is universal. I shall also try to show that all social ethics is derived from individual ethics, and that universal ethics is a dialectical elucidation of individualistic principles. In other words, individualism is axiologically basic.

We should indicate the proposed meanings of good, value, right, and duty. The good is the satisfactory. The satisfactory is anything which causes a feeling of satisfaction, or any experience which contains this feeling. The good also is equivalently defined as anything which is needed. Everyone needs what is satisfactory simply because it is satisfactory. The good is the same as the valuable. It is anything that has value or worth.

There are two kinds of good and two corresponding kinds of value or worth. There is intrinsic good which has intrinsic or primary value, and extrinsic good which has extrinsic or secondary value.

Primary value is the feeling of satisfaction. It is the felt intrinsic satisfactoriness which any experience may have or contain. It, and its opposite, dissatisfaction or intrinsic disvalue, are probably produced by neural processes in the central nervous system. These feelings are not sensations, perceptions, desires, or ideas. They are called, respectively, positive and negative feeling-tones, or positive and negative affects, or pleasure-pain. I do not think that they can be analyzed into simpler experiential elements. Like any ultimate qualities of experience they can be referred to or pointed at. They cannot be described. No one could understand what was meant by the words 'satisfaction' and 'dissatisfaction' if he had never experienced the kinds of consciousness to which these words refer. But everybody has experienced such consciousness. We are immediately aware of all our experience as being either satisfactory or unsatisfactory, and probably almost all is simultaneously both, in varying proportions.

From this meaning of primary value or disvalue it will follow that our theory is an *hedonic axiology*. Feeling-tone or affect (one of the meanings of *hedone* in Greek) is the axiological absolute. It either creates or constitutes the worth and the justification of whatever is worthy and justified. But it is not the metaphysical absolute. While all things depend upon it for their value, still it depends for its existence upon the life processes of a biological organism whose existence, in turn, depends upon ultimate substance or ultimate reality. Feeling-tone is axiologically primary and ultimate, but it is ontologically and metaphysically secondary, dependent, peripheral, and ephemeral.

An intrinsic good, we have indicated, is an experience that *has* primary value. It is any total individual happy experience as of any given moment. It will be a complex *gestalt* including, in many cases, sensation, imagination, desire, memory, anticipation, a rational concept, and feeling-tone. The primary value or feeling-tone is, like each of the other elements, a quality or abstract aspect of the complex total.

An extrinsic good is an instrumental good. It has secondary value. It is a cause of intrinsic good. The secondary value which it has, and which makes it instrumentally good, is its causal relation to intrinsic good.

To summarize:-

(1) Primary value is a feeling of satisfaction.

(2) Intrinsic good is any total experience which has or contains this.

(3) Extrinsic good is anything which causes intrinsic good and value.

(4) Secondary value is the causal relation between an extrinsic good and an intrinsic good.

This terminology, combined with some sound psychological principles, commits us to a radical individualism. Our theory is an *hedonic individualism,* for, all intrinsic goods are individual, since they are complexes of consciousness or experience, which is always individual. The individuality of all experience may be disputed, and it cannot be proved with certainty; but it is indicated by the truth that only a biological organism can be conscious. This too may be disputed. Disembodied spirits, or portions of spirits, might exist. But scientific psychology indicates pretty clearly that all consciousness depends for its existence upon the neurones of a biological organism[1]. Then since such organisms are individual, that is, since they are spatially distinct from each

---

[1]See Brickner, R. M., *Journal of Philosophy*, Vol. 41, No. 9, 27 April 1944; pp. 225 ff..

other, so are people's consciousnesses, perhaps with the exception of any Siamese twins who might have parts of their central nervous systems in common. Barring such abnormalities, consciousness is in every case tied down to the neurones of an individual, separate, and distinct biological organism. Minds never merge or overlap if persons are not Siamese twins, and they seldom or never do even in these linked organisms. Ideas never fly through the air from one mind to another. The 'group mind' is a fiction, unless this phrase means just the interaction or intercommunication of a number of individual minds. Communication occurs, but it is never a direct contact of mind with mind. It is never intuitive. It is always effected through some physical medium. We must reject the theory of mental telepathy which is that one mind can apprehend directly the thoughts of other minds. Supposed telepathy is either an unintentional error, or a fraud, or else it is signalling from a distance, through physical media which are not now understood, and which stimulate sense organs which have not yet been discovered. It is barely possible that electrical currents set up by the functioning of the brain send out electro-magnetic waves which are perceived somewhat as homing pigeons and migrating wild birds perceive and orient themselves to the waves of the earth's magnetic field.

The absolute isolation of all minds or souls from any direct contacts with each other may be called psychological individualism. It means that no person can ever share any experience with anyone else. Spiritually or experientially, individuals have absolutely nothing in common. 'In common' and 'share' mean that two or more people have one thing. Two people can have one physical object. They can own and use a house in common. They can share their candy and pop-corn. But they cannot share their thoughts. Strictly speaking there never were two minds with but a single thought, though there might be two hearts that beat *as* one,—*as if* one. We may speak loosely and vulgarly if we like about people sharing each other's thoughts when they communicate, but we should recognize the inaccuracy of this. We should not try to base upon it any theory that is supposed to be true.

For strict accuracy we must also reject the theory of Platonic universals, the view that one identical universal concept can exist simultaneously or successively in several minds which are located in distinct bodies spatially separated from each other.

This absolute psychological individualism involves the ultimate and absolute axiological individualism upon which all moral obligation is founded. Since experience is individual in its existence, all intrinsic good must be individual. Such good is experience. Also, obviously, all primary value will be individual, being inside an intrinsic good. And instrumental goods and values will be individual, since their axiological significance depends upon their connection with individual intrinsic goods.

Neither axiological nor psychological individualism should be confused with that individualism which means non-cooperation. Axiological individualism implies that men should do what is most satisfactory to them in the long run. This almost always involves a high degree of social cooperation, and depends upon an individual's getting help from others.

This value theory is also in some sense relativistic. Its full name is *hedonic individual relativism*. Instrumental goods are relative by definition. They are things causally related to certain intrinsic goods and values. Secondary value is relative in the sense that it is this causal relation. Even intrinsic good is in a sense relative. This may seem like a contradiction in terms, but at least we must recognize that the terminology of relativism applies properly to it, for an intrinsic good is intrinsically good only in and to itself. It has its primary value inside itself. This value may be known and appreciated by others, but it cannot be felt by them. The only value that an intrinsic good can have to others is an instrumental value. It will have such value to all individuals in whom it causes satisfaction. It will cause this in the souls of all who sympathize with and love the person who contains it. Its ultimate justification or value, from their points of view, depends upon the satisfactions which they feel as a result of it.

Primary value alone is not axiologically relative. It is the axiological absolute.

All good, then is relative. Nothing can be good at all unless it is good for at least some one individual. The good, for him, is always what he needs and what satisfies him. This is always determined by his own individual character or nature. What is good for a canary bird is determined by the nature of the canary bird, and what is good for a man is determined by the nature of the man. Moreover, when something is in fact good for him, there is no logical necessity that it should be good for anybody else. Others may not need it. It may not satisfy them. Their natures may be different from his, either by biological inheritance or by training. His good often is good for others, but that is because their natures are similar to his, or because they love him, or because his well-being enables him to help them.

This relativistic theory does not mean that there is nothing either good or bad but thinking makes it so. Rather the principle is that there is nothing either good or bad but feeling makes it so. We must recognize the affective or hedonic principle as axiologically basic,—without committing ourselves to everything that was included in the ancient egoistic hedonism of Epicurus. We should reject the notion that feeling-tone, the axiological absolute, is or ought to be the goal of all desire and striving. Men can seek knowledge and other intrinsically non-affective objectives as ultimate goals. But the Epicureans were right in thinking that the feeling of pleasure is the ultimate value and justification of whatever is morally justified and worthy. No non-affective objective would ever have any value to a man unless it made *him* feel more satisfied or less dissatisfied. My hedonic axiology reiterates what is true in the ancient, oft libelled, and seldom understood doctrine of Epicurus.

This axiological theory is also in the tradition of the interest theory of value, the essential truth of which is that the chief intrinsic good of any individual is the satisfactions involved in, and resulting from, the fulfillment of his major interests or desires, such as love, ambition, and the desires for truth, for beauty and for sensuous enjoyment.[2] In chapters 6 and 7 we shall describe these major interests in some detail. Perhaps the significance of the abstract principles of the present chapter will become clearer when the persistent motivation by these basic desires is there considered in a more comprehensive manner.

We come now to the definitions of right and duty. These are equivalent terms. One always has a duty to do what is right, and it is always right for one to do his duty. The

[2] See Parker, D. H., Human Values; Geo. Wahr, Ann Arbor, Mich. Pp, 21, 46 ff.

meanings of these terms are to be derived from the meanings which we have already found for good and value. An individual always has a duty, from his own point of view, to attain as nearly as possible his highest good, which is what is most deeply satisfactory to him in the long run. An equivalent statement is that he always ought to do what will meet his deepest needs. This duty is the categorical imperative. It is unconditionally binding upon every individual who is capable of experiencing satisfaction or dissatisfaction. It is universal and absolute. It is a definition. I think that we ought to adopt this definition because it is the only one which will help us the most in understanding man's moral experience. It is the meaning which men use when they speak most intelligibly of right and wrong.

We should note that only the *principle* of duty is categorical. Right *action* is always conditionally right; it is right on the condition that it conforms to the principle. Kant never understood his own theory in this matter of the categorical imperative[3]. If his alleged principle of non-contradictory universality were true, still no act would be categorically right, but only right on condition that it conformed to the principle. Whether or not the universal borrowing of money without the intent to repay would actually stop all borrowing, can be known only *a posteriori*. Perhaps

---

[3]Kant said that an act was morally right if its maxim, the assertion that it ought to be done, could be willed universally without contradiction. Borrowing money without the intent to repay is immoral, said he, because if the maxim were willed universally and thus if all borrowing were without the intent to repay, all lending and thus all borrowing would cease, and the principle that it was willed universally would be contradicted by itself. When Kant's theory is applied to the case where a man refuses to accept a bribe, the result is rather sensational. Would universal refusal prevent all offers and thus all refusals of bribery? If so, according to Kant, refusal would be wrong, for the universalization of the maxim of this act would contradict the universalization of it. See Kant's *Critique of Practical Reason*, 1788.

some lenders would be gullible enough to keep right on lending. If so, according to Kant's principles, such borrowing would be right.

Whatever the ultimately right principle of duty is, it is categorical. Any *act* that is right, is so only on condition that it conforms to this absolute principle. Also all that conform are right. If incest, sadism, matricide, bigamy, and arson were in accordance with it, they would be right, whether the principle actually is Kant's, Paley's, St. Thomas's, Calvin's, J. S. Mill's, mine, or some other. These sins and vices, like all sins and vices, are wrong only because they violate the correct principle of duty, whatever it is.

As I have indicated, I think that the correct principle is the maximation of long range individual satisfaction. This may be dismissed as what has been called psychologism by certain European thinkers. Psychologism in ethics usually means the denial that anything is relevant except those feelings and desires which actually occur in some human consciousness. To conclude that people ought to pursue pleasure or power or fame because they actually do so, is a form of psychologism. Such a conclusion is obviously unwarranted from such evidence. People ought not to pursue anything unless the pursuit, together with its fulfillment, will be more deeply satisfactory in the long run to them than any alternative which they might have pursued. This situation may be diagrammed as follows:

$$X \quad \begin{array}{l} A, A_1 \text{———} An \\ B, B_1 \text{———} Bn \end{array}$$

X has a choice of A or B. Suppose he chooses A; then A_1———An are the consequences. B_1———Bn are what would have resulted had he chosen B. His choice of A is right, from his point of view, if A, A_1————An is more satisfactory than B, B_1————Bn would have been if B had been chosen. The actual experience, motivation, choice and consequences, are not the whole story in determining what is right. X's choice is right only if the thing he chooses, A, plus its consequences, A_1————An, which have not yet happened at the time his choice occurs, and thus which are in a sense non-existent, but which will exist later, must be more satisfactory than B, B_1————Bn, which are non-existent not only in the sense that they have not yet come into existence, but also in the sense that they never will do so. The rightness of X's choice depends upon a comparison of the satisfactoriness of two sets of experiences only a small portion of which, A, exists at the moment of choice. One of these will exist later piecemeal, not all at once. The other will never exist at all. Unless the former contains a greater quantity of satisfaction than the latter, his choice is wrong.

This shows the difficulty of knowing what is right in any particular situation. How can X know which alternative will be most deeply satisfactory in the long run? I think that a man can often know this with a fair degree of probability, but not with complete certainty, by analogy to his own past experience and to that of other people. The bank executive who chooses not to embezzle the bank's funds, knows roughly, by analogy to his own experience, and to that of other people about whom he reads in the newspaper, what would be likely to happen if he did, and what will be likely to happen when he does not.

In conclusion let us note that this individualistic theory implies that there is a plurality of ultimate moral standards, one for each conscious organism, each standard being determined by the individual nature of its organism. What is a duty for one, from his point of view, may be contrary to the duty of another, from the other's point of view; and there is no standard by which either of these duties may be validly proclaimed absolutely right apart from all points of view, or right from every point of view, or right from one absolute point of view. How, then, shall we discover, and how shall we validate, social obligations? I shall maintain that social ethics exists, that it is valid, and that its validity is derived from individual moral imperatives which are ultimate.

CHAPTER IV

Social Ethics

A N individual has a duty to help others if, when, and because he needs to help them. Helping them is an individual moral imperative of his whenever it will satisfy him most deeply in the long run. In his helpfulness he will be, in part, selfish in the ordinary sense. He will help others as a means to getting help from them in return. This is ethical. No moral taint attaches when he pays his debts and respects his neighbors' rights in order to secure services and consideration for himself. Should he omit to give what society demands of him he will be made to suffer. Society can inflict terrible punishments upon almost anybody. Also it can bestow valuable rewards upon those who cooperate. It is constantly rewarding those who have not broken the law, by letting them circulate about freely and say pretty much what they think. It gives thrilling honors and distinctions to those who are thought to have made outstanding contributions. Each individual ought to try to cooperate and to make a creative contribution, partly because he needs to avoid social penalties and to enjoy social distinctions. He needs these rewards because he will be dissatisfied if he does not get them, and because he will be deeply satisfied if he does get them.

This duty of altruism based on ordinary selfishness involves an imperative to maintain beneficent social institu-

recreation
art
science

tions. Casual and transitory social relationships are usually insufficient to give one a satisfying existence. Social relations should be stabilized by active participation in the basic organized institutions of state, family, economic group, school, and church. These groupings have their roots deep in man's cultural past. Discriminating persons in all ages have known how much individual happiness depends upon their preservation and improvement.

A man's duty to help others is, then, based partly on his ordinary selfishness. It is also based partly on his ordinary unselfishness, benevolence, or love. His love aims ultimately at the welfare of others. When love is combined with the sensuous desires of sex and with a few other things it is called romantic love. But it may exist independently of sex, as in mother love or in the brotherly love which has always been the leading principle of Christian ethical teaching. A's love for B is a desire, located in A's soul, whose objective is B's welfare, considered, not as a means to any further end, but as a final goal. A's desire, so to speak, terminates upon its object B. A's love is satisfied when A can help B to be happy and when A knows that B is happy.

Successful love always satisfies the lover. A mother enjoys caring for her children and knowing that they are well-off. She does not aim at this enjoyment. She aims at the children's enjoyment. But the joy or satisfaction which she feels is the intrinsic value of her love to her. From her point of view she ought to lavish her loving care upon her children because she enjoys having them happy. The *cause* in this *because* is not Aristotle's final cause; it is his formal cause. Her own joy is not her goal. But by definition it characterizes what she ought, from her point of view, to do. Her joy (or her escape from suffering) must occur either in her

34

present experiences of child-caring, or in experiences of hers resulting from these, or in both, or else caring for the children is not, from her point of view, her duty. It still might be her duty from the children's points of view, or from society's points of view, if her child-caring would satisfy them more than her not caring, but not from her point of view if she were not more satisfied or less dissatisfied. In such a case as this, of course, society had better try to inflict some punishments on her so that caring for the children will actually turn out to be more satisfactory, or less unsatisfactory, to her, than not caring for them. And society usually does try to punish parents for grossly neglecting their children. So far as it succeeds it gives the parents a duty, from their own points of view, to care for the children.

The primary value or joy which a mother normally feels in providing adequately for her offspring is purely selfish in the sense that it is part of herself. Her love, too, is purely selfish in the sense that its expression is her self-expression, and that its satisfaction is her self-satisfaction. But this is not the ordinary meaning of selfishness. This is a Pickwickian selfishness which consists in being and in expressing one's own individual self. Ordinary selfishness, on the other hand, consists in pursuing one's own future welfare and self-expression as a final objective. Pickwickian individualistic selfishness is absolutely inescapable as long as one lives. No man can desire or enjoy anything unless it is his own self that desires and enjoys it. And clearly no moral taint is necessarily involved in this.

In caring for others by reason of selfish prudence, one is selfish in both the ordinary and in the Pickwickian senses. In caring for others by reason of one's love, one is selfish only in the Pickwickian sense.

Love as well as prudence implies a concern for the maintenance of beneficent institutions. Any rational individual desires to preserve and strengthen these, partly for the sake of the welfare of those people other than himself who chiefly compose them and benefit from them.

Let us reformulate the ultimate principle of duty so as to include the compelling social obligations which are binding upon each person because of the needs of his own nature. Every individual has a duty, from his own point of view, to attain as nearly as possible, (1) his own maximum satisfaction in the long run, (2) that of those whom he loves, to the extent that he loves them, (3) that of those who will help him, to the extent that they will help, (4) that of those who will cooperate with his institutions, so far as they will cooperate. But clearly his duties, from his own point of view, to attain the second, third, and fourth items, are all due to the fact that these things will be satisfactory to him. They are all obligatory, from his point of view, because of the first item. All duty to others is ultimately analyzable into a duty to maximize individual satisfaction.

We should distinguish between the *motivation* for helping others and the ultimate *principle* of the obligation to help them. Love and selfish prudence are the only possible motives. Love seeks the welfare of others as an end. Prudence seeks it as a means. There are no other ways of seeking it. These motives are sufficient when sufficiently enlightened by reason. It is good to help others because we want them to be happy,—because we love them. And by reason we may often succeed in helping, and avoid injuring, those whom we are thus trying to aid. It is also good to help others because we want them to help us in return. An adequate selfish prudence is reason itself applied to the problem of getting the most out of life for one's self, partly by helping others. These motives are not the principle of duty, which is maximum long run individual satisfaction. Motivation is not synonymous with obligation. One need not always pursue one's own long range satisfaction. One ought always to attain it, but this may often be accomplished most nearly or most adequately by pursuing something else. In a good life a man will sometimes pursue his own satisfaction, but sometimes he will forget about it in the pursuit of other goals, such as the welfare of a friend or the truth about nature. A person may be motivated by a desire for anything at all that he is in fact interested in, whether it be internal to his own experience or external. But his obligation, from his own point of view, is always a matter of what his own internal feelings are and will be and might be. Aristotle and Epicurus have misled the western world into thinking that the highest intrinsic good or value must be identical with the goal of all rational striving. The principle that the highest intrinsic value may be achieved by pursuing some other objective has been called the paradox or hedonism; but the only real contradiction here is that this truth contradicts what Aristotle and Epicurus said.

All of the people in society generate just as completely autonomous moral authorities as any one particular individual does. Their satisfactory experiences are intrinsically valuable to them in the same way that his are to him. And the social value of his behavior depends upon their satisfactions. Social value, however, is always secondary value. The social value of a man's love for his children is its causal relations to all of the satisfactions which it produces, directly or indirectly, in other people. If his loving care helps to make his children happy it has a certain social value to them. If it

37

helps to make them useful citizens, it has added social values to many other people who are helped by his children, and some of whose happiness thus results, indirectly, from his parental affection.

Society is also very important because of the imperious demands which it makes upon every individual member, and because of the tremendous power which it exercises over individual satisfactions, to back up its demands. Society requires that each individual make certain contributions, and that he conform to laws, mores, and folkways. We have already referred to the fact that it often makes individuals happy who contribute and conform, and it often makes individuals miserable who do not. But axiological individualism is in no way impugned by the tremendous social influences brought to bear upon individuals. Society's demands are only the demands of individuals seeking what will satisfy them. A social demand, say, that a bank official shall conform to the rules about handling other people's money, is more accurately just a lot of individual demands that he do so. Each of the individual citizens is interested in having the banker conform. If the banks fail the citizen suffers. Each citizen demands the conformity of the banker largely for the sake of his own safety, prosperity, and happiness. In this he is being ordinarily selfish. He also demands it because of his love; he knows that conformity will tend to make the banker and many other persons happy. Also the banker ought, in most cases, from his own point of view, to conform, because that will tend to satisfy his ordinarily selfish interests and his love, thus tending to make him more safe, prosperous, and happy.

Society's power is shown, further, in the fact that it has created every individual. Each one is made what he is by other people. His parents start him off with his body and his biological heredity; and they, and many others, mold his character culturally later on. But even though a man is made what he is by society, still what is right or wrong, from his point of view, depends immediately and ultimately upon what he is, no matter how he got that way. So far as society makes him a happy person, it is instrumentally good from his point of view. So far as it makes him miserable, it is bad for him.

Although society is very powerful, still its might does not essentially or necessarily make anything right. Society's power to punish an individual and make him miserable, does not necessarily make his misery good for him. A man's misery is good for him only if it causes him to be more deeply satisfied later on. Sometimes it does this. It may give him a deeper understanding of himself and of his fellows, strengthen his character, and discipline his spirit. It may broaden and enrich his life, and thus help him eventually to triumph over the obstacles which otherwise would block his path. This is the redemptive power of suffering. But the fact that the force of society or of anything else imposes the suffering does not guarantee the blessed eventuality. Force may, of course, make the right exist or cause it to prevail. A social order which is right for those who benefit from it, is caused to exist by force. It would be destroyed by its enemies if force were not used for its protection. But force will sometimes make the wrong prevail. Not force, but maximum long range individual satisfaction, is the only essential characteristic which formally, necessarily, and universally makes a thing right.

The tremendous power which society wields is exerted in the endeavor to bring each individual's right into conformity with society's demands. When it rewards a man for doing what it approves, it makes his doing this very satisfactory to him, and thus, in most cases, right for him. When it punishes him, for doing what is a wrong to it, it makes this wrong also wrong to him, for his act thus brings suffering to himself. But there are exceptions to this. Sometimes it fails to reward its friends and to punish its enemies. And even when it succeeds, by rewards and punishments, in making social cooperation right for any individual, still this is only Aristotle's efficient making or causing, not his formal or essential making or causing.

Moreover, when society thus succeeds, its success is directly attributable to the nature of the individual involved. Society cannot reward an individual unless he needs what it can give. It could not reward a man who found no joy in honor or status or wealth or security or love. It could not punish an individual who was indifferent to any attempted punishment it might seek to inflict. It could not torture him unless he was an organism capable of experiencing either mental anguish or sensory pain. It can execute him, but if that is just what he desires most, his death will be, from his point of view, a reward and not a punishment. Society can hold a malefactor up to public contempt, and if he does not care he is not being punished. Of course he may say that he does not care, when he really does care and when he really is being punished. Society, then, has moral authority over an individual, from his own point of view, only through his own feelings and his own individual character,—only through his need of society, his love for its members, his prudence, his capacity for being punished, and his capacity for being rewarded.

Some think that if this individualistic theory were true it ought to be concealed so as not to discourage all beneficent social reform. Also it has been suggested that the Russians ought not to be told about it.[1] They might be led to think that they were right from their own points of view in their aggression against the West.

But actually the truth of hedonic individual relativism ought not to be concealed; for it is the only proper basis from which to justify social reform. Take, for example, the problems of war and peace. It must be admitted that a successful war might be a benefit to most of the people of a nation. It would be, so far as it saved them from slavery or gave them prosperity and freedom. For them it would be good. The same war would be evil to its victims, and possibly to nearly everyone in the defeated country, if, as sometimes happens, most of those individuals were enslaved, impoverished, or killed. Then the freedom and prosperity which the victorious power achieved might help to launch it on a career of aggression which might end in disaster for itself three generations hence. Then its original victory will have been good for most of its citizens who were there at the time, but bad for most of their descendants in the third generation. What is good for the individuals of one generation, may be bad for those of a later one in the same country or in any other country. However, so far as people are not satisfied with a system which protects them, but threatens disaster to their descendants, that system is bad for them.

It should be clear that a federal world government ought to be set up. Probably most people now, and in the future, would live more satisfactory lives if this were done, with

---

[1]See paper by Brand Blanshard read at Second Inter-American Congress of Philosophy at Columbia University, December 1947. Published in *Philosophy and Phenomenological Research*, March, 1949, Vol. 9, No. 3; p. 511.

representative democracy, with considerable local auton-
omy, and with safeguards of individual freedom. Then from
most people's points of view such a state ought to be created.
This state would work hardships upon some who have vested
interests in nationalistic separatism and aggression. For
them, the added satisfactions, if any, from world peace,
would not compensate for the added frustrations. From their
points of view a world state would be evil. Then it is our
duty, from our points of view, to inflict this evil upon them,
and to crush their opposition by force if we must, and if we
can, because to do so would be more deeply satisfactory to
us in the long run.

The clash of individual axiological standards comes out
very clearly in crime. Consider the case of a dangerous felon
who has been properly sentenced to life imprisonment for
murder. Here the highest good of most of the law-abiding
citizens demands his incarceration. He must not be allowed
to get away with murder. His punishment is required in order to help protect the lives and property of nearly all.
Moreover his punishment might be the best thing in the
long run for him. Should he escape, worry and a bad conscience might make him more dissatisfied than if he had
stayed in jail. Also it would injure society, and he would
have to live in society; so it would injure him. But, on the
other hand, his punishment might not be best for him. I
think that there are cases where escape would be more satisfactory in the long run for such a felon. A life lived in the
open might be happier, in spite of some worries and pangs
of conscience. It would injure society and thus injure him
to some extent, but it might benefit him more. If so, to escape would be his duty from his own point of view, even
though it would be wrong from most of the citizens' points of

42

view. If maximum individual long range satisfaction makes duty for decent people, it does so for rascals also. It does so for all conscious organisms. The principle is universal.

CHAPTER V

Universal Ethics

THERE are three senses in which ethics is universal.[1] Each sense is a dialectical development from the ultimate principle of hedonic individual relativism, that everyone has a duty, from his own point of view, to attain his own maximum long range satisfaction. The first sense is, as we have already seen, that this principle is itself universal by definition. It is the categorical imperative. It states what is unconditionally binding without exception upon every single individual who is capable of experiencing satisfaction or dissatisfaction.

In a second sense universality is present in ethics, in that, from the point of view of any one, all things universally without exception ought to help him because he needs their help. All of his needs for satisfactory living ought, from his point of view, to be met. From a citizen's point of view a felon ought not to escape, and everything in the universe ought to conspire to prevent him from escaping. But from the culprit's own point of view he ought to escape, and everything and everybody ought to help him, if that would be more satisfactory to him in the long run. Of course a normal citizen will repudiate this latter obligation because it is not imposed upon him by his own point of view. He

---

[1] See my paper in *Journal of Philosophy*, June 24, 1943; Vol. 40, No. 13, pp. 348 ff.

knows that, as St. Thomas says, he must be true to his own highest good, which is God. Also the criminal will repudiate the duty created by the citizen's need. In this ultimate conflict of categorical individual duties, involving, obviously, war in heaven, force determines what is done on earth. The power of organized society will have to be exerted in order to inflict the legal penalty upon the culprit. Force, we have seen, does not determine essentially what ought to be done. The battles of the gods, that is, the final conflicts of human ideals, are not settled by force. They are not settled. The ultimate brittle good of one individual contestant may be in grim, tight-lipped, and unyielding conflict with the ultimate brittle good of another individual.

Understanding this second kind of universality is the key to understanding the whole theory of hedonic individual relativism. Men often grasp vaguely the truth that from their own points of view the whole universe ought to further what will be most deeply satisfactory to them; and then they unwarrantably infer that apart from any point of view it ought to do so. They have not yet fully understood that the highest good of one individual may be contrary to the highest good of another.

Some may erroneously insist that, according to my radically individualistic ethics, a citizen's need that a criminal should stay in jail cannot impose upon the criminal himself any binding obligation.[2] The citizen's need and right and duty are a matter of the citizen's own feelings. The criminal does not feel these. Then how can he be obligated by them? His duty is to satisfy his own long run need and to do what

---

[2] See article by A. C. Garnett, and my reply, *Journal of Philosophy*, July 21, 1949; vol. 46, No. 15, pp. 469 ff., especially p. 471.

is most deeply satisfactory to him in the long run, or so it might seem according to my theory.

But the truth is that employing my definitions, and properly elucidating them by an accurate dialectic, the citizen's need does impose an obligation which is genuinely binding upon the criminal from the citizen's point of view. The obligatory, from the citizen's point of view, is what is most deeply satisfactory to him in the long run. To be satisfactory means to cause or to contain satisfaction. The criminal's staying in jail would *cause* satisfaction to the citizen. It would make his life safer and more prosperous and happy. Therefore it is obligatory from the citizen's point of view. If the walls of the prison all fell down, the criminal still ought, from the citizen's point of view, to stay where he is and wait for the authorities to fence him in again. The criminal will, in most cases, repudiate this obligation if an opportunity offers to get away, because, from his own point of view, he ought not to stay. But when he runs away he is repudiating a genuine and binding obligation which actually applies to him,—from the citizen's point of view. Such an obligation, imposed by the hostile need and interest of the citizen, may have no influence upon the criminal's behavior. But from the citizen's point of view it ought to have.

And this works both ways. The need and right of the criminal, from his point of view, to escape, will have no influence upon the behavior of any sensible citizen. It is hostile to the citizen's good. The citizen will repudiate the criminal's point of view, just as the criminal will repudiate the citizen's point of view. These mutual repudiations, however, should not blind the inquiring ethicist to the existence of both points of view, and to the relativity of all good and evil to some point of view. The ethicist will usually be a citizen himself and will side with all other responsible citizens against the criminal. It would be as morally perverse for him to endorse the criminal's point of view, as it would be intellectually perverse for him to deny its existence or to deny the values and moral obligations created by it.

This theory will seem shocking to some in that it appears to justify a criminal in the commission of his crime. Escaping from jail is a crime, and a criminal is right, in a sense and under certain circumstances, in escaping. But let us go further and apply the theory to a still more horrible deed. Consider the case of a sadist who takes a fiendish delight in inflicting ghastly tortures on his victims. My theory implies that he would be right, in a certain sense and under certain conditions, in his cruelty. Indeed he would be morally culpable if he neglected a perfectly safe opportunity to practice it!

But the sense in which he would be right is 'from his own point of view'; and the circumstances are, that it really satisfied him most deeply in the long run. It would not be right from his victims' points of view, nor from the points of view of any who might sympathize with his victims. It would be right from hardly any point of view,—if from any at all. The actual practice of sadism probably would not be right even from the point of view of the sadist himself. It might satisfy at the moment. He would not do it if it did not do this. But in view of the social condemnation when it is suspected, and due to pity, love, and conscience in his own soul, and due to the likelihood of getting caught, the more extreme forms of sadism are not likely to satisfy anyone in the long run. Some of the lesser degrees of cruelty do thus satisfy some people,—perhaps most people. But hardly the extremes.

For the sake of testing our definition of duty in the most

difficult circumstances imaginable, let us suppose that some extreme sadist would be most deeply satisfied in the long run by his cruelty! Probably this does not happen. But suppose that it did. Society would then have an obligation, from the points of view of its more responsible members, to try to restrain him by force, and also to punish him. Punishment means making him feel dissatisfied. If society can make him feel dissatisfied enough as a result of his cruelty, that makes the cruelty bad from his point of view. Then, so far as he is rational he will not try to do it again; and so far as other would-be sadists who learn about his punishment are rational, they will be deterred from following their socially vile propensities. And this is what society actually tries to do through its penal institutions.

Suppose it fails! Perhaps sometimes it fails. Suppose that the sadist really is most deeply satisfied in the long run by his cruelty. Suppose that he feels no pity, love, pangs of conscience, or anxiety. Then obviously he is right from his own point of view. But he is wrong from everybody else's. We are dealing here with an ultimate conflict of duties, needs, interests, and ideals. This is the battle of the gods *et les dieux ont soif*! What is done on earth is determined by force. In the supposed case, having the power to injure others, and being urged to do so by a rational desire for his own highest good, he injures others. He does what is best for him and worst for them. They try to prevent but they are not able. It is too bad, for us and for his victims, but such things do sometimes happen in this vale of tears. All we can do is try to devise ways and means to prevent them from happening again. We must never relax in our fight against sadism and other heinous sins and crimes, because they are so unsatisfactory to us. But the necessity of carrying on this fight should not drive us to the intellectual perversity of thinking that anything can be best for an individual which does not satisfy him most deeply in the long run.

Strong objections will still be raised in opposition to this truth. Some deny that there really is any ultimate conflict of individual needs, interests, and ideals. The very influential theological tradition of Plato, Aristotle, and St. Thomas, has sought to teach us that there is only one highest good, or God, for all men and for the whole universe, and that in apparent conflict the actual final good of both contestants is really identical. Sometimes something like this happens. In politics and in industry contesting forces will sometimes injure themselves if they completely vanquish their rivals. Each side needs the other. Labor needs management and *vice-versa*. The Republicans need the Democrats, and *vice-versa*. They are all part of a larger whole upon whose welfare the ultimate welfare of each depends. The ultimate highest goods of each opposing pair are harmonious. Or so it sometimes seems.

All experience nevertheless indicates that some things which are best for one are contrary to the best for another. As I have suggested, when a criminal is imprisoned for life, or when he is executed, that is best for most of the responsible citizens. But in most cases it just is not the best thing for the criminal himself. When we kill 'dictatorial' soldiers, death is not always best for them. When we kill rats, rattlesnakes, and mosquitoes, that is not usually best for them. When we kill sheep, cattle, hogs, chickens, and turkeys in order to devour their roasted muscle tissue, that is not usually best for them.

The belief that there is no ultimate and mortal conflict between human beings, or between any conscious organisms, is obviously the product of wish thinking, now re-inforced by the authority of a powerful theological tradition which was itself created largely by wish thinking in earlier days. Men wanted their own way; also, because of their love, pity, and sympathy, they did not want to think that they were doing real evil to anyone in getting it; and, for the sake of their spiritual serenity, they did not want to admit that forces opposing them could in any sense be right.

This involved the confusion of two basic intellectual categories, the metaphysical and the axiological. The metaphysical absolute or ultimate, that is, the supreme being or substantial core of nature, which ontologically underlies everything else, was erroneously called the axiological ultimate,—the highest good. The identity of these two ultimates was falsely taken for granted. Entelechy was confused with hypostasis in a spirit of emotional exaltation, delusive optimism, and intellectual chaos. In simpler language, it was thought that God is all good and all powerful, and that he does not allow ultimate conflicts to occur.

The truth is that there is only one divine spiritual principle, the principle of the individual's highest good, the principle that that good is what is most deeply satisfactory to him in the long run. But this principle implies individual relativism. The highest good of each individual is determined by that individual's nature, and there is no logical necessity that what is best for one will also be best for any other. So, while, as Plato said in the *Timaeus*, sec. 37, and as most alleged monotheists have agreed, there can be only one eternal abstract principle of divinity, still there are many gods, in each of which it is logically contained. The highest good of each individual is his particular divinity, by which standard he should measure his every action, and to which ideal he should give the last full measure of devotion. The particular gods or ultimate ideals are distinct for different people, and not all of these are harmonious. As I have suggested, there is war in heaven, due to the many divergent forms into which biological and cultural evolution have been directed by the supreme being.

Another objection to the truth, that a rascal may be right from his own point of view, is based on the erroneous supposition that if he is in any sense right then decent people ought to approve and condone what he does. Should not good people be in favor of everything that is right? The answer is No! They must be true to their own highest goods. From their points of view they ought to destroy some or all of the goods of a hostile organism. They must do what, to it, is evil. They must repudiate the obligations which its need imposes upon them.

Universality is present in ethics in a third form, in that the truth about every individual good and value is, like all truth, absolutely universal. This will be seen if we compare two assertions.

Criminal A says truly (I) "It is *false* that (X) this punishment of A is good for me."

Citizen B says truly (II) "It is *true* that (Y) this punishment of A is good for me".

In the first assertion we have labelled as sentence X the words, "this punishment of A is good for me", and in the second assertion we have labelled the same words as sentence Y. Then it may seem as if sentences X and Y are one proposition, and that this proposition is true for citizen B and false for criminal A. But nothing that is true for one can be false for another. Strictly speaking nothing is ever true for or against anybody. A proposition may be true *when*

51

someone asserts it, and if it is, then it will be true on every occasion when any body asserts exactly that proposition. This is the universality of truth. A proposition is the subjective meaning of a sentence. It is the meaning which somebody has in mind. It is a truth if it refers to an objective situation and corresponds to it. This situation is the objective meaning of the sentence.[3]

Sentences X and Y express different propositions because the last word "me" has a different meaning in each. It means criminal A in X and citizen B in Y. Proposition Y will be universally true in the sense that whenever anyone asserts exactly that subjective meaning or proposition, namely, that "the punishment of A is good for B", it is true no matter who says it, and, indeed, no matter what words are used. It might be expressed in several ways in English, and it might be expressed in another language. Moreover, assuming that the criminal would be better satisfied if he escaped, proposition X is universally false in the sense that whenever anybody asserts exactly that meaning, it is false.

Thus we have seen that in three senses good and duty are universal; and at the same time, in another sense, without contradiction, they are purely individual, relative, and thus obviously subjective.

However they are also genuinely objective in another sense, namely, that they are real independently of anyone's cognitive ideas about them.[4] What actually satisfies an individual need is good, whether or not anybody knows that it does so. The good is the satisfactory, and some things really

---

[3]See my paper on "Absolute truth and the shadow of doubt" in *Philosophy of Science*, July 1948; Vol. 15, No. 3.

[4]What I am saying here is also expressed by P. B. Rice in *Jl. of Phil.*, Vol. 40, No. 1, Jan. 1, 1943, p. 14.

are satisfactory. Some things cause satisfaction and some experiences contain it. To cause it or to contain it is to be satisfactory.

CHAPTER VI

Persistent Human Motivations — The Major Interests and Desires — Love

I — Desire and Duty

WHAT is best for a canary bird is determined by the nature of the canary bird and what is best for a man is determined by the nature of the man. The essential spiritual nature of a man is *desire*. A desire is any interest, conscious impulse, passion, appetite, lust, wish, will, hope, yearning, or aspiration,—such as an ambition for social distinction and success, a desire that one's children shall be happy, the impulses of hunger and sex, or a desire for knowledge. The *gratification* or fulfillment of desire is the pursuit and attainment of its objective or goal. This produces in an individual's experience a *feeling of satisfaction* (primary value) and makes his total experience an *intrinsic good*. The maximum possible long run gratification of his desire would produce the maximum long run satisfaction, the attainment of which is his ultimate *duty* or categorical moral imperative.

This is never fully attained because there are always some external obstacles which cannot be overcome, and because many of the desires located within one self interfere with each other. The gratification of a man's desire for wealth and power may conflict with his acquiring knowledge or looking after his children properly. A man *is* all of his desires. If he desires power and knowledge, it is the same 'he,' self, or ego who desires both. In case they are in conflict, the highest attainable good, for him, will involve a compromise which gives him the maximum net satisfaction or the smallest net dissatisfaction. He sacrifices as little as he can of himself in order to realize the greatest possible self-expression or fulfillment.

Herein we discover that the formal principle of his highest good is harmony. His duty demands that he make his various desires help each other as much as possible and hinder each other as little as possible. His self is a more or less imperfectly organized, integrated, unified, harmonized system of interests or desires, whose maximum long run joint gratification would involve the experience of his highest good. His categorical imperative, then, will be to attain this harmonious experience (not necessarily to pursue it). One major function of his reason is to make the integration and harmony of his diverse interests more perfect.

Some feeling of satisfaction or primary value may occur apart from desire, probably for the most part in sensuous experience, as when one unexpectedly comes upon the lovely vision and odor of roses with no antecedent desire. But a desire for their continuance is likely to develop very soon. It should be obvious that almost all feelings of satisfaction come through the gratification or fulfillment of desires.

Whether satisfaction comes through desire or without it, an individual's highest good is still what is most deeply satisfactory to him in the long run. It does not matter, from an individual's point of view, how he is satisfied, so long as, in the long run, he is satisfied.

II — Major and minor interests

Desires vary tremendously, though gradually, on a scale from those of major significance to those which are extremely minor. Major interests are stronger than minor ones. They are more enduring and more frequently recurrent. Their gratification is more satisfying. It is more difficult or else it is impossible to find an adequate substitute for them. There are hundreds of minor interests and a few major ones. The major ones are mostly constellations or complexes of similar and related minor ones. A number of minor ones can unite into a major one in the same way that the major ones integrate together to form the supreme personality interest or integrated self.

Many lists of major interests have been drawn up by psychologists and others. A list of basic human needs amounts to about the same thing, for what any organism needs chiefly is that its desires shall be fulfilled. Any list must be somewhat tentative. Possibly several differing lists will give equally valuable insights into the deeper motivations of the human heart. Also there will be some variation of actual interest from individual to individual, and from culture to culture. I shall suggest a list of major interests which is only slightly variant from that offered in D. H. Parker's *Human Values*[1] (pp. 46, 127).

There are, it seems to me, at least nine interests of major importance in nearly every normal human being. These are as follows:

    1—Love or benevolence toward others.

    2—Ambition; the will to power; the desire to be loved, honored, obeyed, and perhaps feared.

---

[1]Pub. Geo. Wahr, Ann Arbor, Mich.

3—The wish for self-preservation, health, and strength.

4—The desire for sensuous pleasure and "physical" comfort.

5—The conscious impulse to play.

6—Curiosity; the desire for knowledge.

7—The desire for beauty.

8—The desire for efficiency.

9—The desire for harmony or formal correctness.

Without a vivid awareness of how the life of man is pervaded by these major interests, students may find it more difficult to apprehend the truth of the abstract principles dialectically elucidated in chapters 3, 4, and 5. It is in the actual experience of the fulfillment and frustration of these interests that we find the verification and the application of the abstract principles. This experience is man's moral experience. Let us then inquire into the nature, the strength, the limitations, the persistence, the ubiquity, and the variety of forms assumed by love, ambition, self-preservation, curiosity, etc..

III — *Love or benevolence toward others*

1—*The nature of love*: We pointed out in chapter 4 that this gentle passion aims at the welfare of others as its final goal. It must be distinguished from selfish prudence which often motivates helpfulness to others as a means to some form of one's own gratification or satisfaction. Sometimes a person is concerned about his fellows at least partly in order to derive a benefit for himself. He helps them in the hope that they will thereby be induced to help him, or to avoid injuring him, in return. This is selfishness in the ordinary meaning of the word. When kept within reasonable limits it is often beneficent. There is no justification for a wholesale condemnation of it. It is probably a factor in nearly every case where one man helps another. But it is not love, which is probably also present in nearly every such case. Selfish prudence and love are usually mixed. When a man knows about others, and when he and they can cooperate, he would usually prefer that they should be happy, partly because that will help his own selfish aims, but also partly because it will help theirs. He sympathizes with them and wishes them well.

His love interest demands that nearly every child on earth shall enjoy life and grow up to be a happy and successful citizen, and that nearly every adult human being shall prosper, and that many of the lower animals shall live contented lives. He will also desire that most of the men and animals in past ages shall have been happy. He will be sorry to learn that many of them suffered so much. And he will desire that most men and animals in future ages will be happy. Perhaps his concern for the present generation and for the next half dozen or so generations is likely to be much greater than his love for those to come in the extremely remote future. He may also have a kindly wish for all living things, if any, on the planet Mars or elsewhere in the universe, as well as for gnomes, fairies, and angels, if he believes in them.

This constant love motivation is ignored by many critics of the abstract theory outlined in chapters 3, 4, and 5. If duty to others depends upon our love and our need of them, then we have no duty if we do not happen to love them or to need them. But a man normally loves and needs nearly everybody. Social obligation exists in fact because of this. The love, need, and obligation are not whimsical, occasional, ephemeral, or transitory. They are basic and persistent. They are of the essence of human nature.

Love, like every other interest, is basically instinctive. A human being is just naturally a loving sort of organism. Many of the lower animals are too. Dogs are affectionate brutes. Love has been developed by biological evolution as a survival factor. Living organisms have often triumphed in the struggle for existence against hostile forces, animate and inanimate, because they have helped their comrades. This has encouraged their comrades to help them, and all have survived better. Prudence, based on reason and knowledge, has led to some cooperation among men, and perhaps, to a slight degree, even among some of the lower animals. But, owing to the weakness of reason and foresight in man as well as in the lower animals, an inherited impulse to love, an innate enjoyment of helpfulness and an enthusiasm for it, has also been needed in order that the species should survive. Where variations and mutations have provided this, natural selection probably has often preserved it and accentuated it from generation to generation.

Human culture and tradition have in many instances strengthened the innate urge. Man has, by reason, understood better than any other species, the value of cooperation, and has taught love to his children. The original instinctive impulse has been developed into a habit, and has been reinforced by social approval and social pressure. An individual is expected to love certain other people, such as, for instance, his parents, his wife, and his children. If he gives evidence of not doing so, he is often subject to social condemnation.

2—*Pickwickian selfishness and self-interest in love*: We have already seen in chapter four on *Social ethics* how love is purely selfish in the Pickwickian sense that it is always a part of an individual self or person, that its expression is his self-expression, and that its satisfaction is his self-satisfaction. This in no way interferes with its being absolutely unselfish in the ordinary sense that it aims at the welfare of another person as its sole ultimate objective. It is double-ended. Every interest is double ended. Every interest has a source and a content in a self, to start with; its later end is its objective. Failure to distinguish the two ends has led to untold confusion in discussions of selfishness and self-interest. Every interest is selfish and every interest is a self-interest, considering its source and its content; that is, in the Pickwickian sense. But love at least is not self-interest or selfish in the ordinary sense since it aims at the happiness of others. Aristotle and Epicurus have misled us, as I remarked in chapter 4, by assuming that whatever is the supreme value must be the final goal and objective of all rational desire. Their great authority has imposed upon us a tradition which it is hard to break. The supreme principle of perfection and of man's highest value, Aristotle's unmoved mover and Epicurus's maximum of pleasure, is the goal of man's rational striving in some of his more illuminated moments. This striving is religious aspiration, and is the true essence of religion. No desire ought to violate this principle, but many desires will not aim at it.

The Pickwickian selfishness of love does not necessarily involve any taint of sin. Love is good so far as it is satisfactory. Moreover, whether sinful or virtuous, Pickwickian selfishness is absolutely inevitable as long as we are alive and awake. Every single interest is selfish, and all interest is self-interest, in this sense.

Strictly speaking love can never be *disinterested,* since it is one of the noblest and strongest *interests* in the heart of man. Popular terminology calls it disinterested because "interest" connotes "selfishness", and love is not selfish in the ordinary sense. But we had better drop this terminology in view of the important ethical insights afforded by the interest theory of value outlined in the present chapter and the next.

3—*Love should not be wholly impartial;* We should never seek to be wholly impartial or equal in all of our loves. Impartiality is possible and legitimate only to a limited degree. Sometimes it is commendable to have an equal love for all of the members of a group, as, for instance, all one's children. But this is really partiality for them as against those whom one does not love so much. An impartial love for all of one's fellows would be partiality for them at the expense, perhaps, of the lower animals and of one's self. An impartial concern for all conscious organisms including one's self would be pure impartiality. But it does not occur and it ought not to occur. One does and one should have a special love for one's husband or wife, for one's parents, and for one's own children. Also one should have a special love, probably different in degree from all these, for all persons who favor just and humane institutions.

Thus we should limit the application of the principle, often asserted, that according to sound justice and morality every individual should count for one and none should count for more than one. It is true that at elections every adult should have one and only one vote. And in some ways every one has equal rights before the law. But in the serious and sometimes tragic business of making a civilized order operate successfully, some individuals are worth more than others. Some ought to be punished, some ought to be killed, some are merely expendable, some deserve small rewards, some deserve great rewards, and some are indispensable.

It is significant that the Chinese have at times feared lest the Christian doctrine of human brotherhood should undermine family life. This doctrine apparently implied equal love for all mankind; and in the Orient men knew that the family depended upon greater love for certain ones than for others. Actually, of course, Christianity in the West is no threat to family ties. Whatever its avowed doctrines, it does not normally induce people to even try to love all human beings equally. The Chinese ought not to take certain official pronouncements too seriously. In this matter the immortal words of Kipling are better expressions of the true spirit of western culture:

> "E'er they hewed the Sphinx's visage
> Favoritism governed kissage
> Even as it does in this age."

4—*Romantic love*: There are four important elements in what is called romantic love. These are (1) ordinary love or benevolence, (2) sex, (3) ambition, and (4) the need of being corroborated and led.

Plato and Freud have treated ordinary love and sex as one thing, called *eros* or *libido;* but I think that we are dealing with two things which ought to be distinguished. The instinctive sex drive is consciously concerned with sex behavior and with the sensuous pleasure which accompanies it. Sex is not an original impulse to look after the happiness of the partner, even though in its normal expression it is beneficently and intimately combined with ordinary love.

Some may feel that sex is often as much a desire to beget offspring, and possibly an anticipatory love of these, as it is an interest in present sensuous pleasure and in the intimate anatomy of one's partner. But here again we have simply another interest which is often associated with sex by people who have discovered the biological connection between sex and reproduction. Civilized people are likely to beget or conceive their children somewhat intentionally, and to feel a certain anticipatory affection for their offspring before these are born. But this intention and this love are different from sex, and are absent from it when civilized enlightenment is lacking. Many savages are reported to know nothing about the connection between sex and reproduction; and of course none of the lower animals know anything about it. These savages and animals may live normal sex lives, but cannot intend thereby to produce young when they do not know that thereby they are doing so. In primitive tribal culture men usually attribute both birth and death to supernatural forces. Good and evil spirits are thought to determine matters of such importance to man.

Lovers may wish to produce offspring, but their desire to do so is not normally an integral element in their romantic love, even though their sexual behavior, which produces the offspring, is such an element.

The third factor normally present in romantic love is ambition or the will to power. This takes several forms. It is partly a desire to control the life of the other party. It is a wish to lead and to be obeyed. Also it is partly a desire to be noticed, paid attention to, respected, and honored. Beyond this, it usually involves an emphasis upon being noticed and honored *by a person of importance*. A gentleman wants the lady whom he loves to have some social distinction and some publicly recognized excellence of character. A lady wants the gentleman she adores to hold a position of importance in the community.

The ambition, in romantic love, is also, in part, a desire to be loved. Any individual feels futile and lost if nobody loves him. When one loves another person in any considerable degree he demands requital. Romantic love will almost always cease in time if it is not returned. Some have thought that this shows it to be purely selfish. But such is not the case. It contains ordinarily selfish elements in it, namely, these various forms of selfish ambition. But genuine romantic love is not just these. It also includes ordinary love or benevolence. The fact that the whole complex phenomenon of romantic love, including ordinary love, will collapse if requital is not forthcoming, does not negate the pure benevolence of the ordinary love. Lovers demand requital. Their romantic love contains selfish elements which demand it. But their ordinary love or benevolence does not. It demands only the welfare of the beloved. By definition, ordinary love is what seeks that objective and that alone. And I think that ordinary love or benevolence is present in true romantic love. But it will cease, due to the way the human mind works, if requital is not forthcoming.

Intimately connected with the desire for requital, and perhaps an essential element in it, is the desire for sympathetic understanding. A man wants the woman whom he loves to understand as much as possible what his desires and hopes and fears are, and to feel as he does about things.

The fourth important element in romantic love, the desire to be corroborated and to be led, is closely integrated with the desire for sympathetic understanding. One wants his beloved to know his inmost thoughts and feelings partly so that she will approve, endorse, corroborate, and sponsor them. He can enjoy them more if she does. Also, in order to believe that he is doing the right thing, he needs to be told by one whom he respects that it is right. In order that he may feel enough self-confidence to enter upon any difficult program of action, and to carry it through, he needs to be assured by some trustworthy person that he is not likely to fail.

Besides mere corroboration of what he has already decided upon, he sometimes needs help from an understanding and sympathetic soul in making up his mind what to do. There are choices, upon the outcome of which his future depends. He may fear to make the decision alone upon his own responsibility. Usually this is due in part to the fact that the other person has experience beyond his own which is useful in coming to a wise conclusion. But it seldom is merely this. In addition, it is because he cannot fully convince himself that either alternative is right unless someone assures him that it is. He needs to be told what to do. He needs to be led. This need exists in his soul along with the other need of taking the lead and giving direction to his partner. These needs may not be in conflict. They may function in different situations.

For brevity's sake, in the above, I have repeatedly said that *he* (masculine) desires or needs this or that; but obviously all of this applies equally to women.

5—*Love and family life*: Romantic love is obviously a major factor in starting new families and in holding them together. Thus it is not only a bulwark of social stability and of human happiness, but also a major factor in promoting other forms of love. In general, love is nurtured chiefly through the cooperative experiences of family life. Several different kinds of love are generated and cultivated in families. Some of these loves function pretty much autonomously. Others are combined with, and in some measure depend upon, one or more non-sexual interests. A mother's love for her young children is instinctive and is largely independent of other motives. Only a major conflict or a disturbance in her pituitary gland can weaken or destroy it. And all of the members of a reasonably well conducted family group tend to love each other because, just by living with decent people, one normally gets to love them.

Also, love combines with various selfish interests, such as pride and the desire for social approval, to promote family cooperation, which in turn usually tends to strengthen love simply by giving it a propitious environment in which to grow. It is a mistake to confuse love with any of these selfish interests, or to think that family cooperation depends on them exclusively without the presence of genuine love. They are extremely influential factors, and one of the chief things that they do is to enable love to flourish more abundantly.

The selfish pride which parents take in a child whom they have begotten is a powerful force making for family solidarity. Parents feel that they have created their child both physically and spiritually. Their self-respect and their sense of their own importance hang on the child's fate. If the child is handsome and successful, they feel that they have done a fine piece of work. If the child should do disgraceful things, they would feel the shame perhaps more keenly than it would. Thus, normally, pride makes them feel an overpowering determination that the child shall amount to something in life; and thus they will go to great lengths in order to protect it and to help it. In this way pride tends to give a higher degree of stability to a family group than is possessed by most social units. Conflicts which would annihilate an ordinary friendship or almost any other social bond, may fail to end completely the cooperation of a family group. Pride is probably stronger than love in a case like this. But love is nevertheless usually present, and is likely to be strengthened by the pride.

Public opinion or social pressure is another factor which tends to hold a family together by making the parents more deeply concerned about their child. Society expects them to take good care of it. Negatively, they feel the sting of social condemnation if they show themselves to be neglectful. In extreme cases the law steps in and imposes fines and jail sentences upon irresponsible parents. On the positive side, society at times accords them honors when they are conspicuously successful in bringing up their children. A woman's social standing in the community may be greatly improved by having a legitimate child or two, and by openly devoting herself to their welfare, as well, possibly, as to the welfare of the father. Moreover the father may enjoy a somewhat augmented social status as a result of his publicly approved domestic arrangements. Thus social ambition becomes a bulwark of family stability and a factor cooperating with love, and tending to strengthen it.

The love of a child for its parents starts in the intimate associations of the home. Living with decent parents it grows to love and admire them, especially when they, for reasons of their own, give it such devoted and loving care. Also, since the child is so dependent upon its parents at first, and perhaps remains so for many years, prudence calls for cooperation, and cooperation produces love. Moreover, especially as it grows older, the love of a child for its parents is bolstered by social pressure and gratitude. Society expects it to be kind to its parents; and genuine gratitude also impels it to requite their loving care. Pride will be a factor, though this will generally not operate as strongly as in the case of the parents' concern for the child. The child tends to be ashamed if its parents do disgraceful things; and its pride in its parents' social achievements will often increase its affection for them.

There is an erroneous popular notion that the fact of parenthood in itself creates a special love of the child for the parents. A child does not love his parents just because they begat him. They have to win his love, with society's aid. The parents' knowledge that they have created the child gives them a pride which tends to produce love. And the child's knowledge that the parents have created it may tend to make it love them, due to gratitude or because it feels that society expects it to love its biological forebears. But a young child will love whoever takes care of it in a kindly way. If an older child is grateful for having been begotten, or if he has learned that he ought to love those who begat him, he will be influenced by these facts to love whoever he *thinks* his parents are, whether those persons really are or not. The *actual* relationship will not influence the direction of his love apart from its influence on his belief about it.

Along with these factors which strengthen love and family ties, there are many things which weaken them. Husband and wife may, of course, decide, for any one or more of a number of well known reasons, that they are through with each other. And it is interesting to observe how many cases of divorce there are in which the affection of parent for child and of child for parent endures. But filial affection in either broken or unbroken homes can also be weakened or destroyed if the parents are too selfish or irresponsible or dictatorial. It can also be impaired or weakened if the child's dependence on the parents proves to be too irritating. And the parents' social achievements may antagonize the child by humiliating it and by arousing its jealousy.

Moreover, the parents' condescending attitude toward the child may also do this. Or the child may be antagonized by the efforts of the parents to push it into a type of work which satisfies them, or which would have satisfied them, while the child is much more deeply interested in something else.

In extreme cases the love which a child normally bears to its parents may cease almost entirely. The child is usually aware that they have taken the initiative in conceiving and begetting it. It knows that the ultimate responsibility is with them. If they repudiate this responsibility or are incompetent to fulfill it, and if they ruin the child's happiness, the child may, if it will and if it can, break away completely. Parents can, and sometimes do, forfeit all rightful claim to further consideration and affection. But the child that persistently refuses to play a helpful part in the family into which it was born is cutting itself off from help which it may need, and which it might secure if it would still cooperate. Parents may be ultimately responsible for their children, but still in most cases they will eventually repudiate all responsibility for a child that proves itself to be utterly and permanently thankless, contumacious, intransigent, and wayward.

6—*The love of humanity; Christian love*: Love, nurtured chiefly in the cooperative experiences of family life, looks far beyond the domestic group. An individual feels a certain degree of benevolence or affection toward all his friends and toward most of his acquaintances and toward those of his relatives who are his friends. Also he will love in some degree every member of any group to which he belongs, such as a club or a labor union or a church or a nation or an alliance or federation of nations. Each member, merely as a member, will get some of his good will. This is perfectly consistent with his having certain antipathies toward certain individual members which may more than overbalance his good will in their particular cases. If he develops an over-balancing antipathy toward nearly all of them he ceases to be a member of the group in any effective way.

A normal civilized individual will usually feel a considerable degree of affection for all of mankind who are willing to cooperate with his institutions. He will be genuinely concerned for the welfare, not only of all of his loyal fellow citizens, but also for all members of foreign nations who either give aid to his nation or at least do not threaten it. And even for his disloyal fellow citizens, for the criminals who break its laws and threaten to undermine its institutions, and for the members of hostile foreign nations who threaten its very existence and, perhaps, attack it, he may experience a very low degree of love. He may feel that, for the defense of his own life and of his own institutions, they should be impoverished or incarcerated or killed, but he may deplore the need of damaging them so severely. Many in the United Nations during the Second World War deplored the necessity of killing so many Germans and Japanese. Furthermore, the average citizen of the United Nations would probably have protested if the surviving Germans and Japanese, or even if their unhappy leaders, had been tortured to death. Such a citizen wants to protect himself effectively from his enemies, even if this can be done only by annihilating them, but he normally loves everything in human form, no matter how evil, at least enough to wish that it should not be tortured to death.

This love toward all mankind is sometimes called *Christian* love, though it is felt and practiced by many non-

Christians, and is not felt or practiced by all Christians. It is *preached* in most Christian churches.

7—*Love and hate*: Unwillingness to torture one's fellows is not a universal human trait. Most people want their enemies to suffer in some degree. In all ages vindictiveness has been so strong, with certain individuals, as completely to wipe out their love of their enemies. All through history some savages and some civilized people have deliberately devised clever instruments for inflicting the most fiendish tortures upon enemies who have fallen into their clutches. People tend to feel this lust for vengeance when they have been exasperated or humiliated, when their own situation is desperate, and when they have not been taught effectively the advantages and the inherent spiritual joys of compassion. Normal people who have been properly brought up, and who are not in a state of spiritual desperation, will be offended when any man inflicts physical torture on another human being. Many who, in the First World War, said that they wanted to boil the Kaiser in oil, and who, in the second World War, thought that they wanted to treat Hitler likewise, would probably have stopped short of inflicting these penalties had they ever actually been in a position to decide the fate of Germany's two ex-war-leaders.

I do not include hate among the major interests because in its more vehement forms it is an occasional rather than a chronic passion. Perhaps it is chronic in most people in its milder manifestations. Hate is, as to humanity in general, a rather significant minor interest. Doubtless there are certain persons in whom it becomes a permanent interest of major significance.

Let us consider three states of the soul in which a person wishes to injure others. First he may wish to damage them

71

merely as a means to defending himself. This is prudence without hate. Secondly he may become angry at others who have deliberately or negligently injured him, and he may injure them in a spirit of vindictiveness or hate. This is normal. And since most people are constantly being injured or threatened in some degree by others, a measure of animosity is likely to be an almost constant feature of nearly everybody's life.

Thirdly, a man may have many such conflicts, and may win a number of them, and may come to enjoy hurting others so much that he will want always to have someone whom he can hurt. He will miss his victims if he has none for a long time. He will be bored if there is no one for him to pester. His cruelty will give him a gratifying sense of his own adequacy and power. In this third case hate has become a chronic need and passion. If it is strong enough it is a major interest. No real substitute for it can be found, and its frustration will be one of the deepest disappointments. It will be stimulated from within the organism. Its demand for expression will not wait till the environment creates an exasperating situation. Certain people, even great souls, do get into this state. Goethe said that he could not be happy unless he was fighting someone. Let us be thankful that this condition can probably be prevented in most cases by proper early training.

8—*Love and cultural creativity*: Man's love of man is a basic motive in much of the creative work that is done in the world. It is not the sole motive, and by itself it is not sufficient. The hard work of the world would not be done if men were moved only by the love of their fellows. Ambition is also a necessary factor, as we shall see in the next chapter. Men labor creatively in industry and politics and science and art partly in order to secure the rewards which society grants to those who, it thinks, contribute largely to its welfare. But they also labor because they desire that others shall be happy. They want to alleviate the distress of suffering humanity and they want mankind to reach a higher level of welfare and prosperity and cultural achievement. They want life to be more interesting and more worth while for the billions of people now on earth and for those who are to come. They are glad that men in past ages were as happy as they were, and they are sorry that there has been so much grief.

A good life, harmonious within itself, and with all its legitimate ordinarily selfish interests finding an adequate expression, is sanctified by its loving dedication to creative and beneficent social aims. Thereby it acquires a value to others which by reflection creates a corresponding intrinsic good or joy in itself, a good that is unique in its elevating influence upon the whole human spirit.

9—*Love for the lower animals*: As we have already suggested, love may be extended beyond humanity to all living things. Some people love their dogs and their canary birds more than they love certain human beings. Mankind often finds a soul-satisfying companionship with certain domesticated animals. In general, however, an animal, either domesticated or wild, will be sacrificed to human welfare if there is real conflict. We kill dogs that bite people. We destroy rats and mice ruthlessly because they menace our health. We destroy dangerous snakes without a qualm. We crush mosquitoes and we poison other noxious insects for the sake of our own comfort and health. Also we kill food animals who do not threaten our lives at all. We cut off little lambs in their youth in order that we may enjoy lamb chops. We devour their broiled or roasted muscle tissue both for the sake of our own nourishment and for our gustatory pleasure.

Not all of us do. There is the vegetarian whose personal love for the lower animals is greater than his gustatory love for their roasted muscle tissue. He may take the lines of Oliver Goldsmith as his slogan:

> "No flocks that range the valley free
> To slaughter I condemn;
> Taught by the Power that pities me,
> I learn to pity them."

And some mystical religions, especially in India, forbid even the killing of insects and poisonous snakes. Mystics may love every conscious organism well enough not to want to kill it. But this seems irrational to most people. Biological evolution has made us the natural enemies of certain species. We and the mosquitoes meet only to poison and to crush.[1] In many of our social relationships with the lower animals, and in some with our fellow men, someone has got to die, and, from our points of view, it might as well not be ourselves.

While the personal love which most of us feel for the lower animals is less than that of the mystics to whom I have referred, still probably all well brought up people who are not spiritually distraught love all living things well enough to desire that they shall not be tortured to death. Let us exterminate rats and termites, but let us avoid inflicting upon them any unnecessary pain. Let us have lamb chops, but let the blows which are struck in the slaughter house kill their poor dumb victims as quickly and as painlessly as possible.

---

[1] See Santayana, G., *Reason in Science*, Ch. 8, Scribners, N. Y. 1905. P. 223.

Love, then, varies tremendously in quantity. We normally have at least a very low degree of it for all conscious organisms, and a much higher degree of it for certain ones.

10—*Love and prudence*: "Prudence" means "rational foresight". There is a *benevolent prudence* which plans the future welfare of those we love, and there is a *selfish prudence* which plans our own future welfare. The former is the servant of love, the latter acts as its regulator. The latter guides love toward some things and away from others, and it decrees that the strengths of the loves, which are directed toward various objects, shall vary. Selfish prudence requires that our love of vermin and of criminals shall be very weak. It has no objection to a sincere affection for animal pets. It usually calls for a much greater love toward members of one's immediate family than toward outsiders. And it usually calls for a stronger love toward fellow citizens than toward foreigners in any case of conflict between these two groups. As we pointed out earlier, whenever one man helps another, he probably does so in part for the sake of selfish advantage as a final end. But this does not prevent him from taking the advantage of others also as part of his final end. The mixture of love and selfish prudence is recognized in the old maxim, "Don't marry for money, my boy, No! No! But marry where money is!" Love can be closely intertwined with an economic motive, and still each motive can retain its own genuine character.

The presence of selfish prudence in all helpfulness has led some people to deny that there is any real love or benevolence in the world. That there is some is, I think, evidenced by the obvious fact that if a prosperous man could, by spending a dollar, save the lives of ten people in New York City or in Central China, absolutely without receiving any honor or advantage for his benefaction and with no fear of social condemnation in case he refused, he would normally spend the dollar. That is, most men love their fellows to some extent apart from any ordinary selfishness. Cynics will reply, he would do it only *because* doing it made him feel better. I would admit that some men might do it merely as a means to their own good feeling and to their better opinion of themselves as the sort of person that society approves. Here the *because* means Aristotle's teleological cause. But some would do it *because* they were glad to act in a helpful manner for the sake of the welfare of others as a final objective. This *because* is Aristotle's formal cause. The gladness or good feeling here necessarily characterizes the helpful act so far as it is successful. Men do not succeed in doing anything without feeling satisfied in their experience of doing it. But this feeling is not always the objective. Some of it lies in the content of the interest, not in the goal. Love, like every interest, is, as we noted above, double-ended. It has a beginning and a termination. It begins in the experience of a self, which is its source. Part of that experience is its content. It terminates upon an objective. We should not confuse its source or content with the end or objective which it pursues.

    11—*Summary*: We have in this chapter tried to show that:

        1—Love is a mixture of instinct and training.

        2—It is absolutely selfish in the Pickwickian sense.

        3—It is absolutely unselfish in the ordinary sense.

        4—Strictly speaking, it is not disinterested, for it is a major interest.

        5—It ought not to be wholly impartial. We ought not to love all men or all living things equally.

        6—It is not sex.

7—Well brought up people normally love all conscious organisms at least to a slight extent.

8—Love should be regulated and guided by selfish prudence.

CHAPTER VII

*Persistent Human Motivations — The Major
Interests and Desires (Continued)*

(I)—Ambition; the Will to Social Power

BESIDES love, we have enumerated eight major interests. Let us consider these in order. Ambition is first.

Ambition is purely selfish both in the ordinary and in the Pickwickian senses. It is a desire to have social recognition and distinction and power for one's self. It is a desire to be loved, honored, and obeyed. It may be a wish to be feared. A man wants his beloved, his relatives, his friends, and many other people to pay attention to him. He wants various individuals to work for him, and others to pay him large sums of money. He wants to feel that *he* has made a large contribution to the social welfare, and he wants to get credit publicly for his good works.

Ambition tends to become extremely competitive. A man measures himself against certain others who are doing the sort of thing he wants to do. His aim is to get more power than they have and to have it show conspicuously in the various public measures of power,—rank, income, impressiveness of the domicile, etc.. Indeed ambition may become almost wholly competitive in certain people who are particularly prone to envy and jealousy. They do not so much enjoy possessing social authority and prestige for itself. What they delight in almost exclusively is possessing more of these than do certain other persons with whom they come to feel a keen sense of rivalry. As soon as one set of rivals has been outstripped they feel lost unless they can find another.

In his *Human Values*, D. H. Parker interprets ambition as being essentially competitive in nature. But I do not think that rivalry is necessarily the predominant factor in what I would call ambition or the will to power. A man may admit that others have powers greater than his own and still he may enjoy the exercise of his own without envying them, or possibly without enough envy of them to disturb him noticeably. Ambition is primarily a desire for social power. Whatever degree of it a man gets he can usually enjoy. He normally desires more but he still may like what he has.

While a man is driving toward power, his ambition forces many serious spiritual readjustments and may prevent inward peace. But it is not necessarily a deeply disturbing element in the soul. Once a reasonable level of social eminence and power is attained the individual may settle into a fairly serene and harmonious routine in which he retains his ambition, that is, in which he continues to feel the demand for social recognition and power, and to enjoy the possession of these, without wishing very strenuously for any more. In such a case a powerful interest is operating and is being satisfied. And I would call it ambition or the will to social power. Possibly some other names might be given to it.

Ambition is selfish in the ordinary sense; but it is good unless it oversteps certain rational bounds. Successful ambition is intrinsically good, because it is one of the most deeply satisfying things in the long run for any man or woman. And it is also instrumentally good. It is one of the major motives for much of the creative and serviceable work that is done in industry, commerce, politics, science, and art. These activities, which serve the life and the spirit of man, would not be adequately performed were it not for ambition. Love is also a factor in all of these pursuits. Men work hard partly in order to help other people. But love is not the only important factor; and love by itself is not enough. Generally men must win distinction through service if they are to serve with enthusiasm for extended periods. Also ambition is a strong moralizing force acting on young people, who are often constrained to behave themselves, by their realization that misbehavior is likely to retard their careers. Also successful ambition may help one to take care of those whom he loves.

Rational selfish ambition is just as moral as love. It is just as important in a good life. It has been neglected by most ethical thinkers in the past because of the over-emphasis placed on love in some aspects of our Christian and mystical tradition, and because men are usually ambitious enough without any exhortations to be more so. Men are often too ambitious and do not love enough. Preachers have often felt called upon to try to tone down ambition and to stir up love, and the ethical theorists have taken their cue from the preachers. But ambition must get its due when we try to give a truthful account of man's moral life.

(2)—*Self-preservation, Health and Strength*

There is no single instinct of self-preservation. There are many instinctive tendencies which help one to save his life.

One has, for instance, an innate tendency to dodge if he sees a blow aimed at his head; also his instinctive hunger leads him to eat food without which he would die. Indeed, most instinctive reactions, except those of sexual reproduction, were originally selected in biological evolution because of their tendency, in near or remote ancestors, to aid in the preservation of the individual so far as that tended to preserve the species. Instinctive reactions are, of course, rough and ready, and sometimes result in self-destruction. Fear has sometimes led people to run away from safe places. Pugnacity has sometimes made people fight when they would have been safer if they had fled. Reason is needed to supplement instinct, and this has been provided also, though in inadequate quantities, as a means to survival.

Rational people, aware of the normal span of life, as well as of its dangers and its values, usually plan to live as long as they possibly can. They have a developed interest in self-preservation which is a joint product of instinct and reason and culture. They deliberately try to keep as healthy as they can. They are constantly taking precautions to avoid accidents and sickness and sudden or slow death in its various forms. The overpowering human wish to live is clearly indicated by the various doctrines of immortality which are found in many religions. Men hate to admit that they will ever die.

(3)—*Sensuous Pleasures and "Physical" Comfort*

This includes the interests in food and sex and rest and such things as hot baths and the scent of perfume and of flowers. The negative form of this interest is the desire to avoid great discomfort and torture. In this latter form it may dominate the whole soul for a time. When an individual is actually being tortured the desire to escape may temporarily take precedence over every other interest.

The terminology regarding pleasure may easily become confusing. Sensuous pleasure must be distinguished from the feeling of satisfaction which occurs whenever *any* desire is gratified, and at some other times besides. The feeling of satisfaction, as we have indicated, is a quality occurring in most consciousness and depending upon neurological processes in the central portions of the nervous system. It is simply the intrinsic experienced satisfactoriness of any total awareness. It, or the feeling of dissatisfaction, or both, are probably present to some degree in all consciousness. They are sometimes called positive and negative feeling-tone respectively. Also they are called 'affects'. They are intrinsic value and disvalue, respectively. They are not sensations. Sensuous pleasure, on the other hand, is quite a different thing. It is a sensation and is largely dependent upon the functioning of some sensory end organ. It is a sensory content which usually has or contains a positive feeling-tone as its intrinsic value. And its opposite, sensory pain or torture, usually contains negative feeling-tone or dissatisfaction. However, cases of masochism are reported where people have inflicted sensory pain upon themselves and have appeared to feel satisfied with it. Some monks have seemed to like mortifying their flesh in painfully ascetic practices. This has given them a sense of purity and of superiority over their despised lower animal natures. Thus an experience of sensory pain can contain the feeling of satisfaction and can be enjoyed and thus can be intrinsically valuable. Also, of course, present sensory pain is often necessary in order to cause a great satisfaction later on. Thus it is frequently valuable in a causal or instrumental sense as well as intrinsically.

The confusion of sensuous pleasure with the feeling of satisfaction has led to a widespread failure to understand both ancient and modern theories of hedonism and utilitarianism, which we shall discuss more at length in chapters 10, 11. Some have thought that the hedonists, chiefly Epicurus, Lucretius, Jeremy Bentham, and John Stuart Mill, meant that *sensuous* pleasure was intrinsic value and the goal of all rational striving. None of the great hedonists believed this in their more lucid moments. They all thought, at least some of the time, that positive feeling-tone or the feeling of satisfaction was intrinsic value, and to this extent their theory is true.

Another possible confusion of meanings is found in the use of the term 'physical comfort'. This means a comfortable sensuous experience which is not physical at all, but psychological. Strictly speaking there is no such thing as physical comfort. A feeling or experience of comfort is a kind of consciousness which is probably called physical because it is produced by such physical things as soft beds, and warm water, and healthy internal biological processes. Though a cause is a physical object, its effect may be a state of consciousness. And no consciousness or experience can ever be identical with any physical object.

It is obvious that sensuous or sensual pleasure can interfere tremendously with other interests when it is exaggerated or when it is given expression under the wrong circumstances. It is always under suspicion in ascetic and puritanical circles. But it is intrinsically good, and when rationally guided and controlled it becomes an important element in nearly every good life. Sensuous delights may be rated on a lower level than intellectual ones, but a complete life must be lived on every level, intellectual, social, emotional, and sensuous. Life is needlessly impoverished if the lower levels are disdained. In the long run it is likely to be extremely unsatisfactory either if an individual tries to get rid of sensuous pleasure completely or if he gives it unbridled expression.

(4) — *Play*

This is probably a separate interest, though at times it is much like art, as when children 'play Indians' or 'cops and robbers' or when they mimic their own family life and 'play house'. In these activities they sometimes present what approaches a dramatic production. Also at times play is like sensuous pleasure, as in swimming. It covers most of men's 'vacation' activities, which are also often called 'pleasure' to distinguish them from the main business or work of life. 'Pleasure' has many meanings.

Play is a form of imaginative interest and satisfaction which is chiefly concerned with imaginative things, and is to be distinguished from those interests and satisfactions which are primarily concerned with adaptation to the real environment and with the control of it. Boys imagine that they are Indians. Girls imagine that their dolls are babies.

Swimming, so far as it is really playful, involves an imaginative enjoyment of freedoms beyond the freedom of motion actually achieved. The real motion is in a measure symbolic of three-dimensional acrobatics beyond those attained. Otherwise it is just sensuous pleasure or a special type of calisthenics. Card players and football players engage in imaginary battles. Sometimes these latter get out of the realm of imagination, and real damage is done. But normally it is all in fun, that is, the conflict is imaginary; both victor and vanquished can laugh together the moment it is over. People can seldom do this after real fights. If anyone can, his attitude toward the fight was playful. The German poet and playwright Friedrich Schiller thought that all life ought to be like sport or play. This, however, is an impossible ideal.

Fine art and religion also find satisfaction in the things of the imagination. Both of these are concerned chiefly with ideals and standards that exceed any actual achievement or real embodiment.

(5) — *The Knowledge or Curiosity Interest*

Man usually desires to know the truth. He has an original instinctive urge in this direction which may be called 'natural curiosity'. Many of the lower animals have instinctive drives of a similar nature. For instance, the study of rats in mazes shows that they tend to investigate new situations and to stick their noses into likely looking openings where there might be something interesting. With man this biologically inherited desire for genuine knowledge can be stimulated tremendously by education and social pressure. The scientific interest is simply a developed form of it.

It can also be discouraged by education and social pressure; and sometimes it should be. People ought not always to have accurate information about things. The public should not learn immediately about the extent of the damage in such cases as the disaster at Pearl Harbor in 1941, because the publication of such information would aid the enemy. Many military secrets should not be divulged. A soldier who is captured should not give accurate information to the enemy which might injure his own troops. If, by lying, he can aid in the victory of a national cause which will further humane social institutions, he should lie. Also certain neurotic people, and some weak people who have long been nourished spiritually on illusory ideas, ought to be continuously deceived for the sake of their own serenity. If some people learn in detail just how their stomachs work, this knowledge will disturb the working of their stomachs. Some people ought to believe in fictions, because to do so will satisfy them most deeply in the long run without injuring anybody else.

But, obviously, in general, the desire for genuine knowledge should be encouraged, and people should be aided in their quest for accurate information. Normal people will be happier in the long run if they know the truth, even though, in this vale of tears, the truth is often very bitter. Usually the more that people can know the better. Correct information which is believed to be correct has intrinsic value, since the experience of it is immediately satisfying. People want to know the truth. Furthermore, it usually has instrumental value, since it is likely to help other interests to success. Knowledge possessed by a man with a good personality usually gives power. Here of course I am making the modern optimistic democratic assumption that human nature is not utterly depraved, but that if it is trusted with real truth as well as with the vote, civilization will probably be improved and in any case will not be seriously imperiled.

Some who reject the indications of reason and science as to truth are really not opposed to truth itself. They generally think that truth will be better attained by following various authorities, intuitions, or hunches, which may have a greater traditional prestige in certain circles.

(6) — *Beauty*

Most people desire that nearly everything, or perhaps everything, shall be beautiful. Each individual ought to make himself or herself just as handsome as he or she possibly can. If one cannot be handsome, at least one should be neat. People want their contours, their colorations, natural and artificial, their physiognomies, and their clothing to be beautiful; also their places of business, their homes, their furniture, their books, fountain pens, and automobiles, the streets of the village or city, and the public buildings.

Men may be content with some ugly things when the effort and expense required to beautify them would be too great. It may be better for certain people at certain times, if their energies are limited, to devote themselves chiefly to ambition and love and health and play and knowledge. But even so they will almost always wish that things looked well and sounded well.

The fine arts are like play in that they satisfy chiefly through imaginary objects. The actor who plays Hamlet does not necessarily in real life hate the actor who plays his step-father. The conflicts and triumphs expressed in a symphony are not conflicts with real opponents or triumphs over real victims. The landscape depicted on a canvas is not a real landscape. While both fine art and play deal chiefly with imaginary things, still the former is to be distinguished from the latter by possessing a higher degree of formal correctness. This is secured by careful planning. Play is usually more spontaneous and haphazard. If children 'play house' thoughtfully enough they may enact a drama and thus create a work of art. We shall consider this subject more fully in chapter 15.

(7) — *Efficiency. Technology.*

Whatever a man does, he takes pride in doing it efficiently. He wants to be skillful. He does not want to be wasteful in attaining his ends unless he is motivated by a particular interest in impressing his fellows by his capacity for conspicuous waste. And one who is thus motivated will probably behave wastefully only in certain public activities, and will strive for efficiency elsewhere.

(8) — *The Interest in Form; Harmony*

The supreme formal principle of all rational experience is *harmony*. This is basic in art and in all of the rest of life. It is the principle that every element should help every other element as much as possible and should clash with others as little as possible. Contradiction and conflict are naturally depressing. People develop an interest in harmony if they are rational and if they have had some experience. Intelligent people try to harmonize all aspects of their lives. We shall discuss this subject more fully in chapter 15 on art.

(9) — *The Indispensability and Imperfection of Each Major Interest*

A human soul is similar to an automobile in one respect, namely, that every major element within the total organism must be present. An automobile which is complete except for the steering gear, is useless. If the pistons are removed it will not run. Nor will a normal personality run properly if it has all of the essentials except health, or all except ambition, or all except love. Achievement and power are almost worthless without love. Love is almost worthless without achievement and power. Life is intolerably impoverished unless every major interest functions satisfactorily.

On the other hand, no essential element needs to function at 100% efficiency either in an automobile or in a personality. The steering gear may be slightly worn, but we can still steer. The pistons may be a little leaky, and they still may have a lot of push in them. All pistons are a little leaky. And so with the soul of a man. No major interest needs to function 100%, that is, none needs to be completely successful. And usually none is. Love is frequently in some measure disappointed. Hardly a man ever attains completely his full ambition. He really ought to have more money coming in. The house he lives in may not be a perfect gem of beauty. His wife may not be, either. And, from her point of view, there may be flaws in his character. Also his children seldom measure up to what he expected of them. There is always something to take the joy out of life. There are always obstacles, both internal and external, which cannot be wholly overcome. Every silver lining has a cloud. And yet if all the major interests are present and are functioning around 80%, a man's life may be deeply satisfactory in the long run, and therefore intrinsically good. The almost perfect state of the soul would be plenty good enough for nearly every normal human being. In fact it would be a lot better than what many are actually able, without much despondency, to attain.

(10) — *Selfishness*

Probably every major interest except love is at least partly selfish in the ordinary sense of aiming at the good of the one who experiences it. Ambition and the urge to self-preservation are of course purely selfish. But the desire for knowledge is not always a mere interest terminating upon the truth as such for its final objective. This desire will often be directed toward the end 'that *I* shall have knowledge'. So far as this is what it does, it is selfish. Similarly an interest in beauty may in part seek the goal 'that I shall enjoy this beauty'. There is no contradiction in these interests being partly selfish in the ordinary sense and also partly directed toward impersonal situations. It should be noted that so far as they are directed toward the latter they are neither selfish nor benevolent in the ordinary sense. 'Benevolent or ordinarily selfish' is not an exhaustive classification of human motivations. However, all of these interests must be absolutely selfish in the Pickwickian sense. Selfishness in this sense is utterly inevitable while an organism is alive and awake.

For a clear illustration of an interest which is neither ordinarily selfish nor benevolent, and which terminates upon an impersonal situation as its final objective, let us suppose a man to desire, as some men do, that a tombstone shall stand over his grave for ages after he is dead. And suppose that he does not expect to enjoy it, or to exist at all, after he is dead. If he really expects the stone to stand there later on he will experience an anticipatory satisfaction while he is alive. But this satisfaction is no part of his ultimate goal. The goal, the stone standing over the grave, can cause no satisfaction to him while it stands there, nor can its causal influence operate backwards in time to produce any satisfaction in him before his death. His anticipatory satisfactions are caused by the evidence he has which makes him think that the stone will stand there. He might have conclusive evidence, and he might be absolutely convinced that it will be there, and still it might never arrive. Any evidence as to future events may be misleading. His objective, then, cannot possibly ever satisfy him; also it might never satisfy anybody else, and he might not want it to. Then his desire is not selfish or benevolent, in the ordinary sense. It is what Joseph Butler would have called a particular passion or affection (*Sermons*, 1726, delivered in Rolls Chapel, London).

In conclusion, human motives are complex and curious. It is rash to assert that nobody can ever have some particular kind of interest. After a rash moralist has thus pontificated, an odd person might turn up who actually had such a one. In the theory of ethics it is not necessary to specify exactly what ends people shall or shall not pursue. The important thing is to point out what ends normal people do in fact pursue, and what they usually find most rewarding, and to understand that, no matter what ends they pursue, their highest good is that which gives them the maximum of satisfaction in the long run.

CHAPTER VIII

The Unity of the Personality.

I — *The Experience of Self-identity.*

ALL of the interests which are located in one biological organism are normally united, by the integrative or synthetic action of the nervous system, into one personality, soul, spirit, self, mind, ego, or 'I'. An individual feels that the 'I' or self in every one of his desires is the same person. He may say 'I want all or certain of my fellows to be happy', 'I want to win power and distinction for myself', 'I want to keep alive and well and vigorous', 'I want to enjoy certain sensuous pleasures', 'I want to relax periodically and have a vacation and play bridge or golf or romp with the children and the dog', 'I want to know what is going on in the world', 'I want some or all of my surroundings to have a beautiful appearance', and 'I want to be skillful in my work'. An individual experiences every one of these 'I's' as being the same self, even though they function at different times and in different interests. He thus experiences the complex unity of his personality.

This experience is so obvious and so ubiquitous that one is likely to take it for granted without analysis. But if one reflects he will find in it much to wonder at. The phenomenon is called self-identity. It is sometimes interpreted as if the self were one identical bit of soul substance present in every interest and in every experience of a given organism.

Scientific psychology, however, tends to discredit this notion, and supports instead the view that the unity of the personality is a matter of certain relationships, mostly unique in character, between the multitudinous experiences of one organism. Such relationships might, of course, be *produced by* an underlying spiritual substance, even if the unity of the personality did not itself *consist of* the continuous identity of that substance. But, again, nearly everything in scientific psychology tends to indicate that these relationships are maintained by the functioning of the nervous system, which is an integrated biological organism and which performs an integrative function in the experiences which it directly produces.

Probably neither these experiences as a whole, nor any parts or aspects of them, are an independent substance with identity through time. Rather they are emergent properties of the integrated nervous system. Their metaphysical or ontological status (their status in existence) is dependent, derivative, peripheral, and ephemeral. But they are related to each other in certain uniform ways. These uniform relationships constitute the unity of the personality, and the experiencing of them constitutes the experience of this unity.

The constancy and uniformity of these relationships throughout any individual's life is, of course, rooted in a substance. It is rooted in the complex substance of the nervous system, the permanence of whose structures, as long as the organism is alive, gives to the soul what permanence and integrity it has. The nervous system, and especially the central portion of it, the brain, is the real spiritual substance of man. That is, the brain *is* a substance. It is a structured constellation of energies which are part of the substantial structured energy of the total universe,—the supreme being. And it has spiritual properties or qualities. It is a complex biological substance, and it has emergent psychological qualities. Being 'emergent' means that these qualities belong to the organism when functioning as a whole, but not to its parts taken separately. A single neurone or nerve cell does not have the spiritual qualities of a man. But about fifteen billion functioning neurones, organized into a brain and a whole nervous system, do have these qualities.

By spiritual qualities I mean all the major interests and a few other things besides. I mean such traits as freedom, reason, loyalty, love, and a passion for justice and for truth. These are of the essence of the human spirit. And also, in its essence is included the various relationships which bind its elements together into a somewhat rational and harmonious unity. These relationships are unique experiences of memory, choice, pride, remorse, and anticipation, and also a certain similarity which is perhaps not unique.

First let us consider memory. An individual remembers his own experiences differently from the way in which he remembers what he believes others to have experienced. Once his own experiences existed inside of his own mind and inside of his own biological organism. He had direct access to them. His memory of them refers to them through no intermediary. There is only one link in the chain that connects his present with his own former experience which he remembers. There are two links in a man's memory of what other people experienced. First there was the past cognitive act by which he knew what they experienced. This involved a jump or transcendent reference,—a reference of his cognitive experience to something beyond itself.[1] He never had

---

[1] Here I am speaking in the tradition of Critical Realism. See *Essays in Critical Realism*, by R. W. Sellars, G. Santayana, and others, 1921; also *Scepticism and Animal Faith* by G. Santayana, Scribners, 1923.

any direct access to what was in their minds. He could only infer their mental contents from what he heard them say and from what he saw them do. This inference from his own auditory and visual perceptions produced an idea or an experience of knowledge in his mind at the time. The second link in the chain is his present memory of this past cognitive experience. Thus his memory of their experiences is really his memory of what he thought their experiences were. But his memory of his own experience is a memory of what he once was sure that it was. He once had it present in the mind belonging to his biological organism. He could not have been mistaken at the time. Of course his memory of it can be mistaken. Memory is never the same experience over again. It is another experience which, at a later time, copies the first one. The copy may be accurate or it may not be. A fraction of a second after an experience has happened the memory of it may be wrong. But probably a man makes fewer errors in remembering his own experiences through one link than in remembering other people's experiences through two links.

Choice is the second relationship which we noted as a factor constituting a unified personality. Choice means that a person simultaneously desires to do each of two things, and that he has the power to do whichever he prefers, but he does not have the power to do both. In such a case he always does the one which he prefers. The stronger desire always wins and is always the more satisfactory of the two at the moment. The weaker always more or less gracefully acquiesces in defeat because it is part of the same self as the one which wins, and this self has experienced more satisfaction by means of its defeat. Being able to choose between two impulses means that both are present in one mind. If the two are not synthesized into one mind they cannot meet in a single choice.

There are, we have noted, several other kinds of relationships which help to bind the multifarious experiences of one organism into a unified personality. One of these is a unique kind of *pride* in the past successes which he remembers as his. Another is a unique *remorse* for remembered failures to live up to standards which the self imposes on itself. He has a unique *anticipation* of the future successes and failures of what he regards as his future self. There is also a certain *similarity* of character running through the successive months and years of his life, which is partly due to the fact that the earlier stages are causes of the later ones.

These relationships fail to unify quite all of the experiences of one organism into the dominant integrated personality which maintains itself through most of life. For one thing, much of everyone's infancy is dissociated from his adulthood. Few persons can remember any experiences prior to the time when they were three or four years of age. People vary as to this. Four is perhaps the average age prior to which nothing is remembered. There was, of course, no gap when an individual was actually at this age. There was no sudden change of personality when the child reached the end of the period which he was to forget as an adult. At four he could probably still remember some of the things he did at three, and possibly some that he did at two. And at five he could probably remember some of what he did at four and at three. There was continuity in each step from the infant self to the later self. But the changes accumulated and the links were gradually severed until at last a largely different self was produced. That is, the six relationships which constitute the unity of the personality were mostly severed. (1) Memory was cut; (2) choice is of course always impossible except as between simultaneous desires; (3) the adult is not likely to be proud of the infant's clever sayings and other distinctions, except, perhaps, as he might be proud of his own children's distinctions, (4) nor is he ashamed of the social *faux pas* or other delinquencies of the infant; (5) nor was the infant interested in the future welfare of the adult who would grow out of him; (6) and there is much dissimilarity between the infant of three and the adult. But there is still some personal unity, linking or comprising both infancy and adulthood. This lies, as we have seen, partly in the transitory memories which do in fact span limited periods between birth and the age of five. And it also lies partly in the attitudes and impulses, learned in those early years, which persist as basic habits in the mature personality. There is some similarity of child and adult which is due to the fact that attitudes and impulses created in infancy have been carried over into the later years. The importance of this carry-over of attitudes and impulses is, of course, tremendous. It determines the basic character of the mature person. If the infant does not learn some of the essentials of civilized living before he is five, the resulting adult will have the greatest difficulty in learning these things later on, and he may never learn certain of them.

Summarizing, then, it is fair to say that there is a sense in which a grown man is to some degree the same self he was at the age of one and two and three. But it is also true that most of the links of self-identity fail to span completely the years of early post-natal maturation.

It should be observed that the partial identity of substance in the one continuous biological organism belonging both to the infant and to the adult that grows out of it, does not guarantee a unity of personality including the two. An underlying substantial unity is probably necessary in order to produce personal unity, but such an underlying continuity will not produce this unity in all cases. It will do so only where it generates the relationships which we have specified.

Another kind of partial or total dissociation is night dreams. These largely express submerged impulses and desires which are incompatible with the plan of life established by the dominant personality. But they are part of the individual's psychological make-up, and they force themselves into consciousness in relaxed moments when the comprehensive plan is not being held clearly in mind. They may be wholly forgotten and totally excluded and dissociated from the dominant waking consciousness. Then they would be discoverable only in hypnosis. Or they may be remembered vaguely in waking consciousness and quickly forgotten unless written down. The dominant waking self is not responsible for their frequently scandalous content.

The total or partial dissociations of early infancy from adulthood, and of night dreams from waking consciousness, are perfectly normal. There are also abnormal dissociations of personalities where certain areas of the experience of a once unified self split apart and form two selves, which may take turns in control of the organism, and are likely to be a bit embarrassing to each other. A classic example of this is the case of Miss Beauchamp (pronounced Beacham) described by Dr. Morton Prince.[2] The synthetical function or unifying tendency in the lady's mind was probably con-

---

[2] *The Dissociation of a Personality*, by Dr. Morton Prince. Longmans Green, N. Y. 1905.

genitally weak, and the conflicts of her desires were to her so terrible that she could not keep both sides in mind at once. Instead of meeting in a choice, they were isolated from each other in four distinct selves which took turns in dominating her organism. Two of these were comparatively unimportant. Another retained the bulk of her original personality and was fairly rational. It was her better self. Another, called Sally, included most of her impish, irresponsible, and mischievous tendencies. Sally told the doctor she was present in the back of Miss Beauchamp's mind whenever Miss Beauchamp was dominant (p. 145). Sally knew about Miss Beauchamp's experiences by memory, but Miss Beauchamp did not know about Sally until informed by the doctor (p. 525). Sally deliberately made trouble for her better self. Sally brought spiders and snakes into her room to scare her (p. 161). Once Sally unravelled a knitted blanket which Miss Beauchamp had made, winding the thread in a great tangle around herself and the furniture of the room and the pictures on the wall (p. 162). When Miss Beauchamp came to herself in this situation she had to cut the thread to get out; and she wondered how she had gotten that way! Also Sally once took her for a long walk out of the city and left her there to get back as best she could (p. 162). Sally was more athletic than the better self; that is, the biological organism which they shared was more energetic when Sally was in charge. Psychological inhibitions in the soul of the better self impaired her bodily strength temporarily. Dr. Prince finally succeeded after several years in resolving some of her conflicts and in merging her several selves, thereby enabling her to regain her normal spiritual unification and integrity.

This dissociation was not quite complete, for, as we said,

Sally knew by memory what the better self was doing. But enough of the unifying relationships were broken to establish two pretty clear cut personalities where there had been only one before. All of the relationships which we have specified must be present in order to maintain genuine personal unity and integrity. If any are missing there is at least a partial split, for, as we have pointed out, unity is *constituted* by these relationships. If self-identity were the simple unity of a spiritual substance it is hard to see how two or four distinct personalities could occur. But many cases of this sort of dissociation are reported.

The importance of personal identity as a survival factor in biological evolution was clearly revealed in Miss Beauchamp's case. Her dissociations interfered very seriously with the practical business of living.

It should be noted that these cases of insanity are only extreme examples of tendencies and events which occur in all normal individuals. Complete dissociation is abnormal, apart from dreams and infancy. Incomplete dissociation happens frequently. We are all mild cases. A man says to himself "You should not have done that." One partly dissociated self is talking to another one and condemning it. Immersed in certain of our activities we may tend to forget about our other interests. Each major interest claims the whole energy of the organism for itself. Love claims all. Play and athletics sometimes claim all. Ambition claims all. Health may claim all. Art may claim all. Also parts or combinations of what would normally be unified major interests claim all. In some men at certain times liquor claims all. The craving for drink may alternate at fairly short intervals with a passionate devotion to one's family.

In these conflicts the warring elements are constellations

of interests or desires. Each element is unified into one integrated subordinate self. Every normal total personality, the
whole spiritual individual of one biological organism, comprises many such subordinate selves often partly at war
with each other. These selves may deliberately injure one
another. In some men a domestic self hates a drinking self
and deliberately tries to spoil its fun. Also the drinking self
may hate the orderly processes of domesticity which op-
press it, and may deliberately interfere with these. In this
sense a man can do deliberately what he knows is evil from
his own point of view, using 'his own point of view' loosely
to mean the total spiritual individual including all of his
subordinate selves. But he can do this only because his soul
is partly dissociated. It is not in human nature for a wholly
integrated self intentionally to do what it knows is injurious
to itself, that is, what it knows is wrong from its point of
view. Nobody ever chooses an alternative which he knows is
less satisfactory to his then self than another alternative
which he could take. A self can injure itself only through
ignorance. In this sense, as Socrates said, vice is folly; and
this is what Socrates meant. Plato has expressed this idea
very clearly in the *Protagoras*, sections 351-358, where he
presents a masterly defence of egoistic hedonism. But Plato
here fails to take account of the conflicts within a total personality. He wrongly assumes complete integration of each
human individual. Also he assumes that 'right from one's
own point of view' is equivalent to right in general. He ignores the fact that an individual can intentionally do what
is wrong from other people's point of view. He naively
assumes that since there is only one ultimate principle of
duty which applies to absolutely all individuals, therefore
the actual ultimate duty of one person cannot clash with

101

the duty of anybody else. This optimism probably flows in part from his metaphysical rationalism and seems to me quite unwarranted.[3]

In normal people the synthetic function of the nervous system and of the soul usually abates these internal conflicts in time to prevent major disasters. The supremacy of the total plan of life is re-established. The plan prescribes that there shall be a time and a place for everything important, that everything important shall be kept in its place and shall function at its proper time, that less important things shall be kept in their places, and that unimportant things which are inconsistent with the big important ones shall be excluded. The life of reason reasserts itself and the total long range happiness of the individual, through both the immediate and the foreseeable future, is in a measure protected. The continuity of the unified personality through past, present and future is recognized and correctly evaluated, and its major demands or imperatives are respected. Provision is made, or at least attempted, for a future enriched by the fulfillment of every major interest, and the present is controlled so that it may some day function as a satisfactory past from the points of view of each major interest and of the personality as a whole.

2 — *The Supreme Personality Interest, the Plan of Life and the Idea of the Total Self; the Interest in Harmony.*

In man, rational foresight and rational retrospective appraisal are generally developed to such a degree, along

---

[3]This discussion of conflicting selves in a normal personality, and of the *Protagoras*, is based on a paper entitled "The highest good and the divided personality," by Assistant Professor Hazel E. Barnes, Department of Philosophy, University of Toledo.

with the remarkable experiences of personal identity, that, as we have indicated above, a single supreme personality interest is produced which comprises all of the interests of the organism, and which may at times take their goals jointly as its goal, so far as their goals are compatible; and which may also at times take their highest joint satisfaction as its goal. Its maximum fulfillment is that individual's categorical imperative. It employs reason, to whatever degree the organism can generate reason, in formulating a *plan of life* which aims to guide the interests in such a way that they may attain the highest fulfillment possible through mutual assistance and reinforcement, and through the reduction of mutual interference to a minimum. It aims to maintain the integrity of the total pattern of the personality for the sake of the maximum satisfaction in the long run. Throughout the entire personality it seeks to enforce conformity to the formal principle of harmony. It aims at what Aristotle meant by happiness and what the hedonists and utilitarians meant by the maximum of pleasure and what others have meant by maximum self-expression, self-realization or the actualization of the essential self. It compels the sacrifice of one interest when it judges that that sacrifice will produce a greater satisfaction in the long run for some other interest and thus for the total personality. The self can endure somewhat cheerfully the defeat of a lesser interest since the self is experienced as, not only the defeated interest, but also the other greater interest whose fulfillment is secured by means of this defeat. So far as the self is integrated and rational it will never knowingly and voluntarily submit to mere sacrifice without any compensating gain. That would be waste.

The total personality interest is brought vividly to the

forefront of consciousness only in reflective moments of spiritual illumination. These are often induced by crises, but also by prayer when that is at its best. The true function of prayer in religion is to remind one of the ideal of a perfect fulfillment of his total self or personality interest. God is this ideal. At ordinary times the experienced self is much more restricted. However, relevant portions of the total plan are remembered in lesser moments. The plan exercises an almost constant guiding influence in the lives of reasonable people.

This plan is the positive side of what sociologists have called the idea of the self, which is a man's idea of what he essentially is, and which implies in a positive way what he wants to be. It is his idea of what his total career should comprise. There are certain things which he could hardly bring himself to do. The plan excludes these. If he ever did them he would experience remorse to his dying day,— unless he changed his plan in a spiritual conversion so as to include them. And there are certain things imperiously demanded in his plan. He feels that he must do them before he dies. To fail would be the deepest spiritual tragedy for him,—again, unless the plan were changed.

His plan requires that he shall be the sort of man who will express adequately his essential nature and his deepest desires. He wants to be the sort of man who will make a long range success of all his major interests. And, very significantly, he wants always to have been this sort of person, and he wants always to be it in the future; making allowances, of course, for the defects of immaturity, the weakness of old age, and other unavoidable limitations. Herein the unity of the personality through time is made evident.

Sociologists rightly point out that the idea of the self is developed in social contacts. We get it largely or wholly from our interpretations of other people's attitudes toward us. We want to be the kinds of persons that others whom we respect want us to be. But sociologists do not always sufficiently emphasize the fact that we are able in some measure to select, in accordance with our own original predilections, the ones who are to influence us. Savages have their relatives and fellow tribesmen inexorably thrust upon them. They must respect these no matter what happens. But civilized people to a considerable extent select their business associates, their friends, and their relatives-in-law. Also they can usually escape from their blood relatives if the need is urgent. Some others determine our plan of life for us, but we decide in part which others shall do this. We respect in some degrees most socially influential people about us, but we respect certain ones a great deal more than others because they are the ones whose ideals are in accordance with our own natural predilections. Thus our own original nature is the primary factor in determining indirectly through social influences what our duty shall be. It steers us into the way of certain social influences and out of the way of others.

3 — *Retrospective, Consummatory, and Anticipatory Interests.*

Due to the unity of a human personality through time, every one of the nine major interests which I have enumerated, as well as the supreme personality interest itself, has in addition to its consummatory aspect whose objects are present, a retrospective and anticipatory aspect whose objects are in the past and future respectively. Or we may say correctly that these aspects are themselves subordinate interests which are included within each major interest, just as each major interest is included within the total personality. However each aspect rates as a major interest itself, because it is permanent and is so deeply satisfying, and because it has no adequate substitutes.

(1) *Retrospective Interests.*[4]

A retrospective interest is a desire that something shall have happened in the past. If the thing did not happen that is too bad, for it is now too late for it to have happened. Nevertheless all normal people do desire that certain things shall have happened in earlier times, and if they think that these did happen their desire is satisfied; and if they think that these did not happen their desire is irrevocably defeated.

The satisfaction of a retrospective interest is a good conscience; its dissatisfaction is a bad conscience. A good conscience is necessary for human happiness. A man must be able to look back to a satisfactory career in order to be contented, because he feels that he himself was the person who had that career. Blemishes in it are blemishes in him. Its virtues are his virtues. Bygone achievements, in accordance with his idea of himself, are a permanent source of joy which can never be taken away unless he loses his memory. Whatever ambition he has achieved under his plan of life, and whomever, that he loved, he has helped, he will remember these things with delight. If he has done his work well, and especially if he has won the recognition of others for it, if he has kept his friends and looked after his dependents

---

[4]See Parker, D. H., *Human Values*, pp. 25-26.

and retained the respect of his fellow men, all this will help tremendously to make him proud and happy.

But also the tragedies of bygone years leave their scars on his soul. If a man has failed to do what he has set his heart on he is likely to be oppressed with regret and remorse. This is a bad conscience. He feels that he himself was that man in the past who inhabited his organism and who failed so egregiously. If failure in the past to live up to the idea of the self was bad enough, and if it continued long enough, he may never be quite carefree again, though this is partly a matter of his temperament and of his ductless glands. Remorse, in theological terminology, is a sense of sin. It is the awareness of permanently and irrevocably defeated retrospective interests. It has a demoralizing effect upon people and it can break the spirit of whole societies in times of serious depression, when nearly everybody's past is loaded with disaster, as in the later Roman Empire. A rational and emotional conversion to new forms of major interest, that is, a new social orientation and a new birth in the spirit, usually involving confession to some sympathetic and understanding soul and a sense of having obtained social forgiveness and absolution, can sometimes minimize greatly its paralyzing effect on the will, and liberate new creative energies. But the soul normally carries its scars to the grave. Past events are irrevocable. There is no escaping their effects completely.

> "The Moving Finger writes; and, having writ,
> Moves on: Nor all your Piety nor Wit
> Shall lure it back to cancel half a line,
> Nor all your Tears wash out a Word of it."[5]

Delusions of grandeur can of course modify the effect of

---

[5] Fitzgerald, Ed., *Rubaiyat of Omar Khayyam*, fourth edition, Stanza 71.

sin very materially. So far as remorse is concerned, what a man really did does not matter if his memory is poor enough. The important question is, "What does he remember?" If he did some very bad things and if his memory tells him that these were very good things, he will suffer no remorse. He will be retrospectively happy. In extreme cases, amounting to insanity, memory reverses things completely, and the deluded person is deliriously happy over supposed glorious achievements which never happened. This in itself is good. Happiness or satisfactory experience is the ultimate intrinsic good. However such delusions tend to produce irrational conduct which later on is likely to result in disaster and unhappiness, if not for the one who is deluded at least for most of those who have dealings with him.

Such a falsification of memory is a break in the unity of the self. It is a dissociation of the personality into separate units or subordinate independent personalities. The integrative action of the nervous system has failed to do its work properly, and the real past experience has at least partly broken away from the dominant personality.

The memories of normal people are often pretty accurate. They are usually more accurate than anticipations. At times people would like to fool themselves about what they did, and they find that they cannot do so very much. However, the memories of normal people can play some tricks. The degree to which they can do this depends upon temperament, which is largely determined by the ductless glands and by past emotional experiences. Insanity is just extreme abnormality in this regard. As I have suggested, we are all at least mild cases.

It is important, then, to bear in mind the distinction between the real past and the man's memory of it. The real past is the object of his interest. He wants the real past to have been thus and so. But the real past has no direct bearing on his conscience. The state of his conscience is determined directly by what his memory tells him. Normally this is greatly influenced by what really happened. But there are always extraneous influences acting on memory, especially the various emotions, which may modify it.

This study of retrospective interest shows that it is possible for an interest to function, and to generate intrinsic values, without its having any object. Thus we should not accept the doctrine of Ralph Barton Perry[6] that an object is necessary in order that value shall exist. His slogan, that value is properly defined as any object of any interest, cannot be defended if it is taken to mean literally what it says. A retrospective interest supposedly directed toward a past object or event, can feel just as genuine as any other interest even when, in the case of delusion, it has no object whatever. It may still properly be called an interest, and it may be perfectly satisfied, and it thus may generate and contain a real value. It is trying to refer to an object; it feels that it is referring to one. It simply fails to do so if there was no past event or object corresponding to what it thinks it is referring to.

(2)—*Consummatory interests*

These are interests in things present or thought to be present. A man has a consummatory interest in an apple which he is eating or in the work which he is doing.

Obviously such interests must be satisfied if life is to be at its best. A man wants life, health, comfort, the welfare of those he loves, achievement, and the recognition of his achievement. And he wants these now as well as once upon

---

[6]*General Theory of Value*, Longmans Green, N. Y., 1926.

a time and some time hence. It is unpleasant to be sick and poor and lonely now, even if he was once strong and prosperous and popular, and even if he expects to be so again.

Also consummatory satisfaction at some time is normally necessary for the existence, later on, of retrospective satisfaction. The things people look back to with pride and joy are the past realizations, not the past hopes or the past memories. In order to look back at these with joy they must really have happened, except in cases of extreme delusion.

Anticipatory joys, too, depend in some measure upon consummatory satisfactions. If none of the latter were ever realized, an individual would become hopeless about the future. Men will not work long with bright hopes if they never arrive at any present achievements. Without consummatory satisfaction a man cannot forever enjoy the expectation of future consummations.

(3)—*Anticipatory interests.*

An anticipatory interest is a desire that something shall happen in the future. Its object is a future thing or event. A man desires now that he himself and that various other people shall have and do certain things in the future. He now wants all of his major interests to be successful then, and he now wants those whom he loves to be happy then. He may also now want his enemies to suffer then.

The satisfaction of anticipatory interests is necessary for human happiness. A man must confidently expect that his major interests will be satisfied in the future, or else he will be very miserable in the present. Even though he has his health, his job, his reputation, his family and his friends now, if he expects to lose any of them in a month or in a year or in a few years, and not be able to find satisfactory substitutes, he will become downhearted now. Joyful confident expectation is a necessary factor in making life worth living.

The anticipatory aspects of all the major interests make up what is sometimes called the interest in security. There is no single and separate interest in this, but there are numerous anticipatory desires for future welfare in every field of human activity.

A man's rationally integrated major anticipatory interests are his *guiding* conscience, which is to be contrasted with the satisfied and dissatisfied retrospective interests that, as we have seen, constitute *good* conscience and *bad* conscience, respectively. These anticipatory interests are the forces deep down in his soul which, with reason, give him the content and the form of the plan of his future life, and which command him to act in accordance with that plan, and which forbid him to give way to whims and irrelevant passions. They fix the goals of life, and their power drives each individual toward those goals, so far as he is rational and is possessed of the needed means.

Just as retrospective interests are directly satisfied, or else dissatisfied, by what is remembered or believed about the past, which may not be at all like the real past, so anticipatory interests are satisfied, or not, by what is believed about the future, not by what actually will happen in the future. When a man takes his future success as the goal or object of his present anticipatory ambitious desire, the fact may be that he will be a success in the future. If so, that will satisfy him in the future. But the only thing that can now satisfy his anticipatory ambition is his present expectation of the future success. There is a significant difference

111

between real future success and the expectation of it. A man can expect future success and not get it. Also he may *not* expect it, and still get it.

Similarly, if a man is discouraged about the future, it is no coming failure that makes him miserable, but only his belief that this is coming.

His belief, whatever it is, will probably be based on some evidence. And if the evidence indicates a quick disaster, there will probably be one. But he may misinterpret the evidence or the evidence itself may be misleading. His belief may be quite at variance with the actual facts as to the future. If he expects to die miserably within a year he will feel badly about it now, even if the truth is that he is going to live long and prosper. And conversely, if he expects everything to be rosy in the years to come he is likely to be joyful now, even if in fact he has only a few days more to live.

His present feeling is the intrinsic value of his anticipatory interest, and it is caused by the evidence which he has as to the future, and by his belief about the future, not by the actual future events themselves which are the objects of his interest. *The evidence concerning the future is what has the instrumental value in this situation.* Future objects have no value whatever as long as they are future. The future, now, is utterly worthless, though it may possess tremendous values when it becomes present.

It appears, too, that some anticipatory interests may generate and contain genuine values, even as we saw that some retrospective interests do, without having any objects. A present anticipatory ambition aiming at a secure income and rank in future years has no object if that rank and income will not in fact occur in those years. But the interest is satisfied in the present, not by its object even if it has an object, but by the belief that its object will occur and by the evidence for this belief. If the individual is unexpectedly killed in an auto accident the next week, his anticipatory ambition may still have given him a tremendous spiritual value right up to the time of the accident, even though the interest actually never had any object at all. Thus, again, we see the impropriety of saying with R. B. Perry that 'value is any object of any interest'.

(4)—*The relative importance of retrospective, consummatory, and anticipatory interests.*

Probably young ambitious people usually get more satisfaction from their anticipatory interests than from the others, and probably old people, who have been successful in life, usually get more from their retrospective interests. In middle life, both anticipatory and retrospective interests loom large. Probably throughout most of the lives of civilized people these two types predominate over consummatory interests. There is more fun in looking back on great past achievements, and in looking forward to great future ones, than can usually be derived from the objects one is dealing with at the present moment. Much of life rumbles along in a humdrum routine of seemingly interminable repetitions of working and playing, of getting muddy and washing up, of food and sex, of sleeping and waking, of dressing and undressing, of talking and listening. A lot of it is drudgery or near drudgery, and through it all our souls are lighted by their retrospections and anticipations of stirring triumphs. Of course, we could not enjoy these retrospections, barring extreme delusions of grandeur, if no real triumphs had ever been consummated in the past, at a time when it was present. And we would in time cease to expect great triumphs if none were ever realized in any actual present. Some basis in consummation is normally necessary in order to create deeply satisfying retrospections and anticipations. But these consummations need not occur every few minutes or even every few months. They are spaced at varying intervals, and in between times our spirits are buoyed up by looking forward and backward at them.

In the Pickwickian sense, they are all personal and selfish triumphs. But often they are also unselfish in the ordinary sense. Whenever a man glows with joy at the remembrance of a distinction won by his son, he experiences an unselfish triumph which is also, in a sense, a selfish victory; for it is a victory of his own total self. That is, his retrospective love and pride are both being satisfied. His pride is obviously selfish in the ordinary sense. And in the Pickwickian sense, so is his love. The satisfaction of his love is, tautologically (repetitiously) speaking, the satisfaction of one of *his* major interests.

CHAPTER IX

Time and value

DO the past and the future have value? Did they? Will they? If so, when? and in what sense? Our answers depend upon the metaphysics of time and succession. Human intelligence and human logic are not wholly adequate for an analysis of time. Some contradiction here will prove inevitable. Logic and time are in a measure at war with each other. Zeno the Eleatic showed that absolute logic would eliminate all time and change. Logic deals with eternal relationships. Temporal change in some sense violates eternity. Eternity is a constant reproach to time. And yet both are significant in human experience. We should reconcile them as far as possible, but dogmatic perfectionism here tends to bring on hysteria.

Consider first mere succession. Suppose that A is succeeded by something. Then A is a predecessor only by its relation of precedence to what succeeds it. But at the time that A occurs its successor, call it B, is in the future and does not exist at all. The future will exist, but as yet it does not. For the present it is utterly nothing, just as the past, which once did exist and was then a real present, is now utterly nothing. Then A is a predecessor only in relation to B which is nothing at all. Then is A really a predecessor? 'Preceding' is a relation, and if A is a predecessor only by being related, it might seem that it would have to be related to something. If B is nothing, can A be related to it? Perhaps we escape this difficulty by saying that while A has no successor as long as A exists, still it will have one as soon as B exists. But by then A will be past and utterly nothing, so how can it have any relations?

Also, can 'nothing' really be B's predecessor when A really preceded it?

If A were said to have a successor, B, that is real while A exists, then A and B would be simultaneous, and B would not be A's successor, and we would have contradicted ourselves quite badly. If time is real (which some deny) then (1) B cannot be real when A is, and (2) A cannot be real when B is. We must not deny either of these two statements, for time *is* real. Time is change, and changes do occur. To deny this is folly. It is to fly in the face of experience.

Admitting the reality of time, we may use either of two alternative ways of speaking, neither of which, however, is wholly free from contradiction. (I) We may say that A is a predecessor of B while A exists, in relation to B, A's successor, which is nothing, but which will exist after A has ceased to exist. (II) Or we may say that while A has no successor, still it will have one. It will become a predecessor of B when B exists, and only then,—only at a time when A does not exist any more. Here we are saying that after a thing has ceased to exist it acquires a relational property. If true this would seem to me most remarkable. I prefer the former manner of speaking. I think that while a thing or event exists it has temporal relations with future nonexistent things which will exist.

These same two alternatives are open to us in speaking of successive causation. (I) If A is a preceding cause of B, we may say that it is a cause while it exists, and thus at a time when no effect has as yet resulted. There is no effect, though there will be one after A has ceased to exist. (II) Or we may speak otherwise as follows: Though as long as A exists it has no effect, and thus is not a cause, still it will have an effect after it has ceased to exist and will then become a cause. A would thus acquire a relational property after it had become utterly nothing. I prefer the former terminology. I think that A, a cause while it exists, has a temporal-causal relation with its future and as yet non-existent effect. If A and B are temporally related other than simultaneously they cannot both exist at the same time. But still they can be related temporally as predecessor and successor.

Now let us apply these principles to the causation of value. If A is an instrumental good because it causes B, an intrinsic good, we may ask, when is it such a good? (I) Is it instrumentally good while it exists due to the mere fact that B will result from it later on? Can it be made good at a given time by a causal relation to what is utterly nothing at that time? I think so. (II) Or should we say that A becomes instrumentally good only when B exists and after A has become utterly nothing? Can A take on a new relational property after it has ceased to exist?

I admit the legitimacy, and I assert the partial contradictoriness, of each of these ways of speaking. But I prefer the former.

Note what it implies.

Any event now is instrumentally good by its causal relationship to all of the future intrinsic goods which will actually result from it in all future time, whether these are known and foreseen by anybody or not. While the future realization of a man's ambition is utterly worthless now, because it now contains or causes no intrinsic value, still his present acts

117

which will result in his realization of his ambition ten years
hence are all instrumentally valuable now because of their
causal relation to that future realization which now is nothing. That which is utterly non-existent makes an existing
event instrumentally good. This is not Aristotle's efficient
or final causation. It is his formal causation. That the
future intrinsic goods should result from the present event
is necessary by definition in order that the present event shall
be instrumentally good.

It should be remembered, somewhat parenthetically, that
the only present intrinsic value involved in a man's ambition
for future power consists in the satisfaction he feels now in
believing that he will have the power later on. Also, it
is not the future power which causes his present satisfaction,
and thus which has secondary or instrumental value now in
relation to it, but the evidence he now has which makes
him believe that he will have this power in the future. Obviously the falsity of his belief would in no way diminish
the present intrinsic value of his anticipatory ambition.

Consider the instrumental values of some things or events
in the remote past. Consider the vitamines in the food of
the men of the Renaissance, which were utterly unknown
at the time but without which those men would have
withered and died, and would never have passed on the
torches of life and of civilization to us. All our joys are
caused by the vitamines prevalent in 1550. (I) Did those
vitamines have instrumental value in 1550 as the causes of
our joys in 1950? Our joys of 1950 were utterly nothing in
1550. They were in no proper sense contained in those early
vitamines. The container theory of causation was thoroughly
disproved by Hume in 1739. (II) Or should we say that
these vitamines became instrumentally valuable in 1950 as

causes of our joys in that year, 400 years after the vitamines had ceased to exist? I prefer the former terminology in spite of its contradiction. I think that time, change, and temporal relations are real. The vitamines are really related, causally, to the joy they cause. They *have* the causal relation, while they exist, to *what will follow* as a result of them. The logic here is not wholly adequate, and I do not think that it can be made so. But it is not too bad.

All past events that have contributed causally in any degree, either directly or indirectly, in any degree of indirectness and with any number of causal intermediaries, to the creation of the actual joys of any conscious being, were, when they existed, instrumentally good relatively to those joys. This means that probably all events in the infinite past of the universe were good. Also all that contributed at all to suffering or the loss of joy were instrumentally bad. Nearly everything that has ever happened has been both good and bad on many scores, that is, from many points of view. Also nearly everything that is now happening is both good and bad in the same way. And nearly all future events will be so as long as there is consciousness in the universe. If consciousness should ever cease completely, as for instance if the earth froze up (as it will within fifteen billion years or so) and if everyone died and if there were no life on other planets, and if there were no angels or other spirits, and if life would never evolve again, then after that there would be no more value at all in the universe. But if, after a dead period in which intrinsic good and value were wholly in abeyance, life and mind and consciousness and joy and sorrow evolved again, then most of the events during the dead hiatus would probably have instrumental or secondary value; for they would probably be all, or nearly all, causally related, indirectly, to the later joys and sorrows. Not till intrinsic good and its primary value are finally ended never to be revived will instrumental good and secondary value be ended or even suspended. Intrinsic good can cease temporarily. Instrumental good can only cease permanently.

CHAPTER X

Egoistic hedonism

MY humanistic ethics agrees in a number of ways with the theories of ancient egoistic hedonism and of modern utilitarianism. Also it diverges in part. Let us consider these theories in this chapter and the next.

Ancient hedonism or Epicureanism, in the thought of its two most distinguished protagonists, Epicurus (about 300 B. C. in Athens) and Lucretius (about 60 B. C. in Rome) taught three important doctrines, as follows:

(1) The ultimate nature of things is little hard chunks of material substance, like miniature dice and billiard balls, or like sand or dust, conglomerations of which make up all tangible and visible objects. This is atomistic materialism.

(2) Every man should aim at his own maximum pleasure. Pleasure is intrinsic good or value. Good and value are not clearly distinguished.

(3) The greatest pleasures in life are the absence of pain, and those of tranquillity, philosophy, and friendship. A man should renounce economic and political interests and ambitions. He should cultivate instead these gentler pleasures in the seclusion of a garden with a high wall to keep out the bustle and the battle of life.

This materialistic saintliness of the two greatest figures in the hedonistic tradition is in sharp contrast with the bibulous sensuality of some who later took the name of

121

hedonist and Epicurean, and who popularized a slogan about eating and drinking and making merry because of the proximity of death. Food, drink, and merriment are usually essential features of a good life. But, as all of the important hedonists have understood and said, such a life has many pleasures on a higher level than mere sensuous satisfaction.

(1) *Atomistic materialism*: Nineteenth century physics since Dalton was pretty much in agreement with ancient atomism, which Epicurus copied from Democritos (c. 400 B. C. in Abdera). Both regarded the atoms as ultimate solid chunks. However the physicists a century ago thought that the atoms of different elements such as carbon and iron were intrinsically different in quality. Democritos and the Epicureans regarded them as all qualitatively alike, varying only in size and shape.

Since about 1900 A. D. physicists have remained atomists but have discarded the notion of atoms as *solid* chunks, and have substituted the theory that each one is a miniature solar system with electrons spinning around a central nucleus. The whole structure appears to be a form of the ultimate energy of the universe,—which is not shown by experience or reason to be conscious, volitional, moral, or purposive. These traits in the higher forms of animal life are explainable as emergent products of natural evolutionary processes, biological and cultural.

The ancient Epicureans assumed emergent evolutionary naturalism. They believed that no single atom contained any consciousness or pleasure, but that certain constellations or integrations of atoms did. While they never formulated this theory explicitly as we do to-day, still they should be given credit for a philosophy of naturalism, of evolution, and of emergence,—which principles seem to me to be true and important metaphysical bases now, as then, for a sound humanistic axiology.

It will be evident that materialistic metaphysics has no close or particularly significant connection with what in modern times has been called materialistic or economic motivation, the materialistic interpretation of history, and Marxian dialectic materialism. Actually the desires for economic sufficiency, affluence, and security, are spiritual things. They are aspects of some of the most powerful and basic interests which constitute the human spirit. Obviously they have been important factors in determining the human behavior which has molded history. Their perversions, greed and avarice, still pertain to the human spirit. These are things that have gone wrong with the spirit. They might be called 'unspiritual' in the sense of being 'bad spirit'; but they are in no proper sense materialistic. The great materialists, Epicurus, Lucretius, Hobbes, Marx himself, and Santayana, have been singularly lacking in these pernicious traits.

(2) *Pleasure is the good*: The Epicurean doctrine that pleasure is the ultimate good or value, and that it ought to be the final goal of all rational striving, needs clarification. The word 'pleasure' has many meanings. Besides those of satisfactory sensory experiences (sensuous or sensual pleasures) in contrast with intellectual or emotional experience, and of satisfactory vacation or play experiences in contrast with serious work, pleasure has three meanings of particular importance in ethics. These are:

(1) Feeling-tone; the feeling of satisfaction. This is primary value.

(2) Any total individual experience containing this. Here we have intrinsic good.

(3) Any object (thing) or objective (event) causing these. This is instrumental good.

'Pain', the opposite of pleasure, also has three corresponding meanings. It means a feeling of dissatisfaction, any total individual experience containing this, and any object or objective causing it. Pleasure thus is the good in two senses of pleasure and of good. Also pleasure is in one other sense primary or intrinsic value.

A person's duty, from his own point of view, is always to *attain* the largest possible long run pleasure for himself in the first and second senses (primary value and intrinsic good). He does not always have a duty to pursue these pleasures. If by pursuing truth or the welfare of those whom he loves, he attains the maximum long range pleasure, then he ought, from his own point of view, to pursue these other objectives and not his own pleasure in the first and second senses. However, if he does not pursue his own satisfaction (first sense) or his intrinsically satisfactory total experience (second sense), he *usually* does have a duty, from his own point of view, to aim at an objective which will *cause* the maximum of satisfaction for himself, and thus which will be a pleasure to him in the third sense. The truth which he seeks or the welfare of those whom he loves, will, if he secures or attains them, cause pleasure in him, even if he does not pursue this pleasure. I say that he *usually* has such a duty,—but not necessarily always. If his objective were that a tombstone should stand over his grave after he was dead, he would be aiming at that which would never give him any pleasure. His *expecting*, while he lived, that the stone would stand there later, would give him pleasure while he lived; but his *objective,* the standing of the stone over his grave, could never please him once he was really dead, nor could *its* causal influence work backward through time to produce pleasure in him while he was alive.

In this matter, then, we may agree with the ancient egoistic hedonists only to the extent that it is *almost always* one's duty to seek the maximum long run pleasure for one's self either in the first, second, or third senses. The exceptions, however, are not highly significant.

We may agree with them completely in their conviction that the measure of the value of anything is the quantity of pleasure involved in it or produced by it. Pleasure in the first sense varies only quantitatively. Feeling-tone goes up and down on one linear scale extending from the highest positive feeling-tone, through zero, down to the lowest negative feeling-tone. An object's value or disvalue depends entirely upon the quantity of pleasure or displeasure in the first sense, and in the long run, that it contains or causes.

Here we run into a problem which was raised by John Stuart Mill as to the quantity vs. the quality of pleasure. Mill said that it was not quantity alone which determined value. A pleasure less in quantity but more refined in quality might have a higher value, he asserted, than one which was greater in quantity but cruder. His thought here is confused. But he is hinting at a truth which should be recognized. Pleasure in the first sense of feeling-tone can vary only quantitatively. But pleasure in the second sense of a total individual experience can probably vary qualitatively also. There appears to be sense in saying that some experiences possess more refinement than others. The experience of a symphony concert seems more refined than that of a wrestling match or a burlesque show. Will it therefore have a greater intrinsic value? It will if its refinement involves a greater quantity of feeling-tone, that is, if the individual in the case feels a greater satisfaction. Refinement of pleasure in the second sense may, as Mill said, increase value. But it does so only if it increases the quantity of pleasure in the first sense. If any man were more satisfied with a wrestling match than with a concert, the match would have more value to him. Refinement is worthless to those who do not like it or profit by it.

Refinement adds to the value of a pleasure for most people who have certain inherited abilities or who have had educational advantages, or both. Refined pleasures involve more intelligence, and a greater sensitivity to nuances of feeling and of meaning. But there are some who find that putting so much intelligence into play is a mental strain, and some are lacking in the necessary sensitivity. Perhaps almost anybody can be trained to appreciate refined pleasures, but a person still should leave them alone if he cannot learn to love them without undergoing more grief than they are worth in the long run. If they are not worth while for him, then for him they are not higher pleasures.

Mill thought that the more refined pleasures had a higher value apart from anyone's point of view. He said that the connoisseurs who judge them to be higher are objectively right, for they know both the higher and the lower pleasures, while the judgments of simple people who prefer crudities are discredited by their being unable to appreciate anything except crudeness. In reply we may point out that the simple folk can still be right from their own points of view. If their crudities satisfy them more in the long run than refinements would, they should stick to their crudities. Also Mill gives the connoisseurs more credit than they are always entitled to. They may not be able to appreciate some of the simple pleasures. Moreover, refinement vs. crudity may be a matter of the point of view. Perhaps there are refinements in wrestling, or in anything that anybody calls crude, which the socially prominent music critic is not subtle or sensitive or well-educated enough to appreciate.

The experts and connoisseurs and critics, who tell refined people what they should like, have a genuine authority over all minds which are largely similar to their own or which can become so by training without too much grief. But the experts have no proper authority over low-brows who glory in their so-called crudities.

Moreover, in what is called refinement, a certain value may be sacrificed. More may be gained. On the whole it may be worth while for those who love it. But the so-called simpler and more elemental pleasures have a unique value which we do not wish wholly to lose. Life is usually better and more deeply satisfying if they can be retained, at least in part, when more refined and sophisticated pleasures are added. Sometimes the higher pleasures contain the simpler ones, as for instance romantic love which includes a sensual element in it. But sometimes the higher pleasures exclude the lower. The dignity and pomp, which are never wholly separable from an executive office, may render certain forms of public frolicsomeness inappropriate. We see this principle exemplified also in comparing an oil painting with an etching. The oil has an added richness and a higher value. And yet there is unique value in the black and white of the etching which is lost when color is used. Again, a symphony is richer in value than a piano sonata. And yet the piano has a unique value as a solo instrument. Oil paintings and symphonies should be assiduously cultivated. But also we wish to retain a place in human experience for etchings and for piano sonatas.

Some will challenge the legitimacy of using 'pleasure' in the third sense to mean physical things or objectives which merely cause satisfaction. It will be said that 'pleasure' should always mean a feeling or some sort of experience or consciousness. But a crackling fire in an open hearth on a cold winter night is, properly speaking in traditional English, a real pleasure. It is a pleasure in the third sense because it gives pleasure in the first and second senses. The physical process of eating an apple is a real pleasure in the third sense so far as it satisfies the man who eats. Also the apple itself may properly be called a pleasure in the third sense if it satisfies. Moreover, a child is a real pleasure to the parent who loves it. And the process of caring for it is likewise a pleasure if love is present in the parent. All extrinsic goods are pleasures in this sense, and most objects and objectives are or will be extrinsic goods.

(3) *Epicurean saintliness and defeatism.* In its preachments as to the manner of life by which one is to attain the greatest pleasure or satisfaction in the long run, the ancient Epicureans reflected the decadence of their age. During or after the era of Alexander the Great a failure of nerve and a spirit of escapism set in in the ancient world which culminated during the period of the decaying Roman Empire in the complete other-worldliness of Plotinus (c. 250 A. D.) and St. Augustine (c. 400 A. D.). While the Epicurean theory as to the ultimate nature of value is mostly correct, still the kind of life that the great Epicureans recommended in order to achieve the highest value in the long run is truly admirable only in degenerate societies or in unfortunate individuals. Their saintliness and renunciation were and are slavish

virtues. Their outlook was timorous and apprehensive. In the shipwreck of their political and economic lives they sought to save what they could. One should do this if one is shipwrecked. But in more propitious times and climes normal and healthy minded persons ought not to try to live by the principles which apply properly only to periods of social calamity.

In Epicurus's day the dictators had taken over and many lives were wrecked or threatened with disaster. The basic political and economic structure of society was not amenable to rational control. The government was corrupt and often indifferent to the people's welfare. The average citizen could not exert any influence upon it for reform. It was futile to try to make society just, so that individuals who fully participated in it might live good lives. Wealth and social distinction did not come as a reward for public service. They were prizes that only ruthless and crafty men could seize. Business was in a depression. In general, life was hard, and Epicurus thought that the main thing was to get through it with as little grief as possible. He was on the defensive. His attitude was negative. Great positive social achievement was out of the question. If a man was aware of the finer things in life the best way to keep his self-respect was to retire to a garden and cultivate the things of the spirit,—tranquillity, friendship, and truth. These would prove most deeply satisfactory in the long run. These are, of course, good things. But Epicurus's exclusive emphasis upon them is a serious distortion.

It has been suggested that methodologically Epicurus was an egregiously sentimental philosopher. He is said to have adopted Democritean materialism, not because of any rational interpretation of the evidence of experience, but because of the spiritual implications of the theory. If true, it promised him that for which his weary spirit chiefly yearned; and so he believed it was true! Possibly he also thought that experience, interpreted by reason, indicated its truth. I hope so. I think that experience, interpreted by reason, indicates that the naturalism in this theory is true. I am glad to find him soundly naturalistic. But I hate to see naturalism arrived at by wish thinking.

Wearied by the buffetings of life, the chief thing for which his spirit yearned, and which his materialistic metaphysics promised him, was eventual *death*. Let us not worry, he said; for when this hard life is over it is really over. The dead are really dead. We need fear no punishment or anguish in the next world. Dying may be a bit gruesome just in passing, but death itself is nothing. Once we are dead we are so dead we do not mind it.

Atomistic materialism also gives tranquillity by freeing the devotee during his lifetime from fear of menacing supernatural powers which the uninitiated imagine to lurk all about them.

Materialistic saintliness is too negative for healthy-minded people. It aims merely at the avoidance of trouble. Avoiding this is important but is not enough. Socrates (d. 399 B.C.) and Plato (d. 347 B.C.) had a far more positive, constructive, and inspiring attitude toward life. Plato wrote about how to construct a just social order so that individuals could participate fully in every important social activity and still live good lives. He started a school to train men for social leadership. He passionately sought to grasp the ultimate truth about things by dialectical reason, not by wishing, in the belief that this truth would make men integrated and whole.

In our present generation I think that most of us will get more inspiration from Plato than from Epicurus. While civilization is now faltering slightly, let us not be too downhearted. We have the techniques of representative democracy which the ancients never had. This is no time to dismiss as chimerical the ideal of the beloved community expanded to the scale of a world community.

It is significant that Plato understood and expressed clearly the doctrine of egoistic hedonism. In the *Protagoras,* sections 351-358, he gives the most adequate brief account ever written of the real truth that is in it. He delineates accurately the relation of the individual hedonic factor in axiology to man's highest good and ultimate duty. Virtue, he says, is the knowledge or the correct measurement of the quantity of individual pleasure involved in the long run in any act. He shows by implication that escapism is no necessary element in egoistic hedonism.

Also in the *Republic* his ethics is hedonistic. The basic pleasure theory is explained in book nine, which is less often read than the earlier books. Here (sections 581-583, 586-589) he finally refutes the theory, advanced by the despicable Sophist, Thrasymachus, that the ruthlessness of rulers toward citizens and subjects is best. Plato does this by showing that the pleasures of avarice and brutality are inferior to those of wisdom and the rational harmony of all the major interests. It is too bad that elsewhere, in the *Georgias* and the *Phaedo,* he was so impressed with the real truth of how rational harmony is a necessary factor in the highest good, that he denied the hedonic nature of intrinsic value. Man will, indeed, be unable to attain or approach his highest good without rational harmony, but still that good or any other good is good only because it involves pleasure in the first and the second senses.

In his book *Man For Himself* (pp. 190-191) Erich Fromm says that because of Epicurus's saintliness and failure of nerve, we should not use 'pleasure' to mean the satisfaction which is ultimate in all value, but only to mean those satisfactions which come by taking the easy course and by dodging the tough spots in life. I disagree. Epicurus's escapist aberrations in no way discredit the pleasure theory. Plato expressed this theory better than Epicurus did, and without any *weltschmerz*. Let us avoid Epicurus's world-weariness, but let us admit the correctness of his ultimate theory of value that pleasure is intrinsic value, that it constitutes the final worth and justification of whatever is worthy and justified, and that the quantity of value that anything has depends upon the quantity of pleasure involved.

The traditional, widespread, and fallacious objections to egoistic hedonism are probably due to the fact that leaders in church and state have felt that its general acceptance would menace their institutions. Perhaps it seemed dangerous because of its naturalistic denial of God as a supernatural force who was deeply implicated in human affairs. Perhaps its predominantly Pickwickian selfishness seemed to be a tainted form of egoism. As a result of traditional prejudice it is seldom fairly stated or understood. The basic truths in it are ignored or denied. False, childish, and vicious principles, which Epicurus and Lucretius never expressed or lived by, are popularly attributed to them.

CHAPTER XI

Utilitarianism

THE chief books which have created modern utilitarianism are *The Principles of Morals and of Legislation* (1789) by Jeremy Bentham (1748-1832), *Utilitarianism* (1861) by John Stuart Mill (1806-1873), *The Methods of Ethics* (1874) by Henry Sidgewick (1838-1900), and *The Data of Ethics* (1879) by Herbert Spencer (1820-1903).

These men could see that ancient egoistic hedonism was correct in lighting upon pleasure as intrinsic value and as the key concept in ethics. But they had been deeply influenced by the Christian doctrine of brotherly love and by growing democratic and humanitarian ideas in the nineteenth century. They were revolted at the apparent selfishness of the ancient hedonism. Their effort was to create a social and humane hedonism. They thought that each individual has a duty to aim at the maximum pleasure, happiness, or good of all human beings. Sometimes they included all conscious beings, such as animals and, if any, gnomes, fairies, spirits, angels, gods and demons. In view of the conflict and the necessity of choice as to whom one would help, they often said that we should aim at the greatest happiness of the greatest number of individuals. This is called the principle of utility.

It seemed that this alone, in a hedonistic system, could account for the fact of man's moral experience that an individual is often morally obligated to sacrifice his own personal values for the social good. Sometimes a soldier ought to give up his life for his country. Egoistic hedonism seemed incapable of accounting for this.

But it was hard for the utilitarians to show plausibly and in detail just why an individual ought to aim at the greatest good of the greatest number. Bentham did not try. He said it was so and let it go at that. Mill made two attempts, neither convincing. At the start of chapter four of the *Utilitarianism* he said that each individual desires his own happiness and therefore that the general happiness is a good to the aggregate of all persons. This is the fallacy of composition. If A desires A's happiness, B desires B's happiness, and C desires C's happiness, it does not follow that one desires the happiness of the other two, nor that the happiness of any two will be good for the other one.

At the end of chapter three Mill told another story. He said that the ultimate sanction of the principle of utility is an individual's feeling that his own highest good is consistent with, and conducive to, the highest good of others. This feeling or opinion, said Mill, is reliable. There is no real conflict between people's highest goods. One man's highest good is always best for society. But Mill's sentences here are badly constructed. His rhetoric stumbles because his thought is stumbling. I do not think that he was clear in his own mind about this matter, and I do not think that these paragraphs represent his deep-seated conviction. Surely, in his more lucid moments, he knew that there were ultimate conflicts. In talking about the greatest good of the greatest number instead of the greatest good of all, the utilitarians were admitting there were conflicts. Obviously anybody's feeling that there are none is untrustworthy. Mill's confusion is further indicated by the fact that he ascribed the trustworthiness of this feeling to its being instinctive and not having been trained into us, whereas in his essay on *Nature* he asserted that any instinctive impulse, unmodified by education, was likely to lead us astray.

In dealing with this problem Herbert Spencer admitted that there were some conflicts; and he suggested that these would probably cease in the ideal society with which his cosmic evolution would provide us.

Henry Sidgewick[1] settled the issue, he thought, by some rational intuitions (*Methods of Ethics*, 7th edition, Bk. 3, Ch. 13, pp. 386-387). There is the intuition of *prudence* which tells us we ought to look out for ourselves, the intuition of *benevolence*, which tells us we ought to look out for others, and the intuition of *equity*, which tells us to be fair or impartial with all.

But a rational intuition is obviously a *deus ex machina* and an *ad hoc* invention designed to save a theory which is experiencing its death agonies and crying out for help. The evidence of experience, as interpreted by reason, fails to indicate that the universe which we inhabit is of such a nature as to supply us with these guiding rational intuitions.

Experience, however, does indicate that our moral obligations to help other people are genuine, and are based on love or on selfish need, which the universe has actually created through a process of emergent evolution, biological and cultural. The roots of duty to others, and of all duty, are not rational principles but urgent desires. Reason is needed for the attainment of man's long range highest good. But individual desire and its satisfaction is the ultimate

[1]The term he used to mean Utilitarianism was Universalistic Hedonism.

basis of every genuine moral imperative. Desire is the spiritual essence of man. An individual desires that other people shall be happy, and therefore he will be in some measure satisfied when he is able to help them and when he knows that they are well-off. He ought, from his point of view, to help them because he will be better satisfied if he does. He ought, from their points of view, to help them because they will be better satisfied if he does. Also his selfish need is important. In order to satisfy his other desires he needs to win other people's good will; and he needs to have them capable of helping him. For this he must often help them. He will be better satisfied in the long run if he does. Therefore he has a moral obligation to do so. Individual love and selfish need create a man's duty to his fellows. The whole social duty of man is determined by these two things. Nothing else is needed to make the obligation binding. Reason, foresight, and knowledge are of course needed in order to fulfill the obligation.

Consider the soldier who dies for his country. He has a duty, from the social points of view, that is, from the points of view of the bulk of the citizens, to sacrifice his life because the citizens will be better satisfied if he does. Should he refuse they might come under the heel of a foreign tyrant. The question is, How will these individuals feel? not, What will cause the greatest total happiness in society or in the universe?

Moreover, the soldier may have a duty, from his own point of view, to sacrifice his life for his country. Possibly he would rather die honorably to-day by the enemy's bullets than shamefully to-morrow by the bullets of a firing squad. This is selfish need. Or possibly this obligation, valid from his own point of view, may bind him because dying young would satisfy him more in the long run than living to a ripe old age knowing that he had been a coward, knowing that he had failed to do what certain people, whom he respected, expected him to do, knowing, possibly, that they were aware of his failure to measure up, and knowing that they condemned him for it. Also his love for his country may make him prefer to do what will be helpful to his fellow citizens even if it cuts short his own life.

I am ready to agree with the utilitarians that the principle of utility is generally valid. But it is not the ultimate principle of ethics. Most of the time men have a duty to strive for the greatest happiness of the greatest number. When they do, this obligation derives its validity from the ultimate principle of hedonic individual relativism, to which there are no exceptions. It is meaningless to talk about values or duties unless we specify *for whom*.

The total quantity of value or satisfaction or happiness in the whole universe does not necessarily affect anybody's duty in the least unless he loves everybody in the universe or else unless in some other way everybody's happiness will enhance his happiness, or both. The only thing that counts, ultimately, in any society or in any universe, is the quantity of individual happiness which each individual has. And the only people to whom this matters are the individuals themselves and anybody else who loves or hates them, and anyone whose happiness is in any way enhanced or diminished by their happiness. Thus, of course, each human individual's happiness does matter in some degree to nearly every other human being. But deep-seated conflicts are modifying factors.

Consider the following illustration: suppose that the citizens of a vicious, aggressive, and criminal nation were half as happy, per individual, and three times as numerous, as the people living in free countries. Then their total intrinsic value would exceed that existing in the free countries. It would be once and a half as great. Then if the wicked nation got into a conflict with the free countries so that one or the other of the contestants would have to be almost completely destroyed, in order that its opponent should survive, the duty of the people in the free countries would be to destroy the wicked nation if they could, even though they thus destroyed more value than they saved, and thereby decreased the total intrinsic value in the universe. This would be their duty, from their points of view, because it would be more satisfactory to them in the long run than being destroyed.

Moreover, granted mortal conflict between the two groups, a citizen of a free country would still have a duty to destroy his enemies and save himself and his fellows, even if his enemies, whether more numerous or not, realized a higher average intrinsic spiritual value per individual than was possible in the free country. In a case involving such higher individual values the conflict, of course, would not be so likely to result in the destruction of one of the contestants. With superior individuals a compromise could probably be worked out and mortal conflict could probably be averted. And if the free citizen loved these superior folk, and if he sympathized with them, he would be thwarting his own love were he to help destroy them. But he would still be likely to make this sacrifice if it should be necessary in order to save his own society and his own life, that is, if the conflict could not be compromised and if it were really ultimate and mortal. Supposing that love and sympathy were at a minimum, as they would be should a hostile species of superior beings invade the earth from the planet Mars, man's relationship to them would be like the present relationship of the food animals to man. These animals would be right, from their own points of view, in destroying man, if they could, in order to save themselves from being devoured, even though man is spiritually superior to them and possesses a greater intrinsic value. The destruction of man would, of course, be wrong from the point of view of man, the superior being. And if any animals ever threatened to do this man would probably be able to effect some compromise with them and would probably stop eating them. Universal human vegetarianism is always a possibility.

The principle that the quantity of individual satisfaction, not the total satisfaction in the universe, is always the ultimate criterion may also be illustrated in a population problem. Suppose that increasing the population of the earth tenfold resulted in crowding and in a general decrease in the standard of living and that as a result of this the happiness of all the people was reduced, on an average, per capita, by one half. Then the total quantity of satisfaction, pleasure, or intrinsic value in the universe would be five times as great. But this would be a much worse condition of human affairs than we now have. When individuals are only half as happy as they were, that is bad for them and for those who love them and for all whose happiness is in any way reduced by their decrease in happiness. It does not matter how many of them there are except as this affects the quantity of happiness in each individual's experience. If increasing numbers decreases individual happiness, then increasing numbers is bad for those whose happiness is decreased. If it increases individual happiness it is good, again for those whose individual happiness is increased.

Consider the case of a criminal such as we discussed in

chapters 4 and 5. Suppose that he was put in jail for life and that his good was thereby sacrificed, against his will, for the good of society. Clearly society was right, from its points of view, in imprisoning him, not because the social goods realized were greater in number or in quantity than his individual good, but because the individual citizens were better satisfied having him in jail than *they* would have been if they had let him go. It was not a matter of the total value realized in comparison with the total value lost in him. It was rather the total value gained by each citizen in comparison with the total that that citizen would lose, through social insecurity, if the criminal got away,—that is, from the citizen's point of view this was the issue.

And when the criminal is in fact imprisoned, the citizens show that they have the power, through political organization, to make their points of view, their wills, their choices, their goods, and their rights, prevail. What is done on earth is determined by force. What is right, from the point of view of any individual, is determined by what is most deeply satisfactory in the long run to that individual.

Measuring the quantity of satisfaction

It may be objected not only to utilitarianism but also to egoistic hedonism and to my hedonic individual relativism that satisfactions or pleasures are not strictly speaking quantitative and that they cannot be added together to make any significant total, either in one individual's soul or for all the individuals of society. This has been a stock argument with those who have felt that anything called pleasure must be low and sordid. Henri Bergson, in his *Time and Free Will*[2]

---

[2] English trans. published by Allen & Unwin, London, 1910.

argues at length to prove that no conscious states are properly speaking quantitative at all. He says that when we try to measure experiences all that we succeed in measuring are the physical stimuli which produce them. Take a sound of a supposed given volume or quantity. How shall we double the quantity? We might blow two steam whistles instead of one, or double the steam pressure, or double the velocity of steam through the whistle, or double the force of the impact of the air vibrations on the ear drum. Each of these procedures will have a different effect upon the sensation. Which one really doubles it? Who can say? Doubling the impact is perhaps the most likely one to do so. But doubling the impact will actually have different effects on the sound sensation at different points on the scale from minimum to maximum volume of sound. At which point is the sound really doubled? There is apparently no way of measuring the sound itself. The quantities of different sounds appear not to have any numerical rations.

Bergson insists that quantitative concepts simply do not apply to sensations. What we have called quantitative differences are really just qualitative differences. Loud and soft sounds are different qualities of sound. There is no significant quantitative relation between them.

This same principle applies to light and taste and smell and to all sensations. Bergson thinks that it applies to all experience, and therefore to value experience. If eating one apple gives me a certain satisfaction, will eating two apples give me exactly twice as much? Bergson would say that there is no significant quantitative relation between the two satisfactions. Economists however would say that value experiences are quantitatively related. According to their law of diminishing utility the satisfaction from two apples would really be greater than that from one apple, only it would probably not be quite twice as great. As extra units of any good are added beyond the point of diminishing utility the satisfactions per unit decrease. But economists are in agreement with Bergson to the extent of admitting that the amount of the decrease cannot be accurately measured.[3]

It seems that Bergson has pointed to a real difficulty in measuring the quantities of certain conscious states, but that he has gone too far in denying that these are in any sense quantitative, as well as in denying that there is any way at all to measure any of them. The qualitative differences between loud and soft sounds, strong and weak lights, and great and small joys or satisfactions, are idiomatically and properly called quantitative in all languages. The quantities of these are varied by variations in the quantities of their stimuli. It is true, as Bergson said, that measuring the quantities of the stimuli does not exactly measure the quantities of the experiences. Nevertheless I shall try to show that, by other means, the quantities of some satisfactions can be measured and exact numerical ratios can be shown to hold between them.[4]

First let us note that some satisfactions can be proven to be greater than others. When a man chooses A instead of an alternative B, the anticipation of A in the moment of choice must necessarily contain a greater satisfaction than the anticipation of B. Otherwise he would not choose A. Choice is always in accordance with preference, and preference for A over B *means* a greater or stronger feeling of satisfaction in

---

[3]Anderson, B. M., *Social Value*, Houghton Mifflin, N. Y., 1911, p. 183.
[4]I regret that in an article which I once published in *Ethics* (April 1945; Vol. 55, No. 3, pp. 216 ff.) I denied that numerical ratios could thus be established. Since writing that article I have thought of the way to measure them which I shall explain in this Chapter.

anticipating A. Next let us note that the quantities of two satisfactions can be compared if they are both in one soul and if a conflict arises between them which the individual can resolve only by a choice. It is, of course, essential, in this comparison, that the choice should occur within one soul. And it must really be a choice. If the individual could have had both A and B then their quantities have not been decisively compared. Moreover, in such a case, if each satisfied about equally, he himself probably could not tell for sure which satisfied him more. But if he could not have had both, and if he took A in preference to B, then the evidence is conclusive that A satisfied him more in the moment of choice.

But now suppose that in the moment of choice he realized, as he might, that he would just as soon have B as A. He had to choose, but each satisfied him equally. He chose arbitrarily because he could not have both, and he did not want to lose both. But he felt and knew that he valued each in just about the same amount. Here we have two satisfactions which are proved to be quantitatively almost exactly equal. Then each one is half the sum of the two. Next suppose that later on he must choose between A plus B together, or C, and suppose that his character and his valuations have not changed significantly in the meantime. Also suppose that here again he is indifferent which one he is to take; again he chooses arbitrarily. Then the satisfaction from anticipating A plus B is about equal to that from anticipating C. Then the satisfaction from anticipating A is just about half of that from anticipating C. Here is a numerical ratio between two satisfactions within one soul. And if, by this method, five satisfactions are proved to be practically equal to each other, and their sum is proved to be about equal to a sixth, then each of the five is about a fifth as great as the sixth. Thus numerical ratios of any degree might conceivably be established by arbitrary choices between any satisfactions within a single soul.

There are, of course, difficulties in actually making the measurements. Real choices may not occur involving the satisfactions we are interested in, and if they do, the individual may not be indifferent and arbitrary in any of them. Also his valuations may change between his earlier and later attitudes toward a given object or objective. But if this happened to any considerable extent he would probably know it. And in spite of all these difficulties, the point which I wish to make is still true, that numerical ratios between pleasures or satisfactions are proved by the possibility of arbitrary choices to be *significant*. Bergson and others have said that these supposed ratios are without any meaning or significance whatever. Bergson goes much too far. If the impossibility of *exact* measurement rendered quantitative concepts inapplicable and without significance, such concepts would never have any significant applications at all. For nothing can ever be measured accurately. With the most precise instruments an engineer cannot measure the exact length of a metal rod. There is always a margin of error. But the rod always has an exact length; and all pleasures have exact quantities even though we have trouble in measuring them, and even though sometimes we cannot measure them at all.

Furthermore, numerical ratios are significant as between the satisfactions of different individuals, even though no interests or satisfactions in two individuals can ever meet face to face in a choice. People are pretty similar and their feelings are sometimes quite similar. Two men might be equally satisfied with A. If they were, a numerical ratio of one to one would hold between their feelings about A, at least for the moment. And then any feeling in one man which was one seventh as great as his satisfaction with A, would be one seventh as great as the other man's satisfaction with A. Thus, obviously, all of the feelings of the two men, and of all men, and of all organisms which are conscious of satisfaction and dissatisfaction, are related in exact numerical ratios.

While comparisons of satisfactions between two individuals are difficult, as we have seen, and can never be quantitatively exact, still true comparisons may sometimes be made with an approach to accuracy. Moreover the evidence for such comparative judgments is often very strong, though never 100 percent. As between two men, if one is very happy and the other is very unhappy, this is often very obvious to themselves and to others. They may show by their behavior that there is a great difference in the quantities of happiness which they experience. And if these quantities were about equal, that too could be known. But in such a case there would be no way of knowing exactly which one was greater, since two satisfactions in two souls can never meet and clash in one choice.

The difficulties of measurement, we have noted, are not so great within one soul, and it is interesting that satisfactions can there be added, and dissatisfactions subtracted, and whether the resulting net total is greater or less than another satisfaction or dissatisfaction, usually itself a net total of several satisfactions and dissatisfactions, can be ascertained. If a man has to choose between taking A and B, the anticipations of which satisfy him, together with X, the anticipation of which dissatisfies him, or C, D, and E, the anticipations of which satisfy him, together with Y, the anticipation of which dissatisfies him, and if he chooses A, B, and X, that proves that, at the moment of choice, the net total of the satisfactions and dissatisfactions which he feels in anticipating A, B, and X, is higher or more satisfactory or less unsatisfactory than the net total which he feels in anticipating C, D, E, and Y. This is significant addition and subtraction without the use of any units of measurement. It tells with certainty which net total is greater, though it can give no numerical ratio between the two.

And we should note that the intrinsic value of any individual is the net total of all the intrinsic values or satisfactions and disvalues or dissatisfactions which he experiences. All of these can be and are significantly added and subtracted because of the unity of the personality or self who experiences them. All are synthesized into a unitary value by the integrative action of his nervous system.

Satisfactions and interests are, of course, also numerically expressible in the sense that they can be counted. But counting them is no help in knowing how much value they or anything else are or have. One satisfaction may be greater than the sum of three others, or it may not. The final proof as to which is greater is only by preference and choice.

From this we may conclude, contrary to the contentions of most anti-hedonists, that 'the quantitative total of all value in the universe' is logically significant. The expression has meaning. All pleasures and displeasures add and subtract to form a significant net total. But this total does not necessarily have any moral significance. Even if anybody loves everybody, still he will probably have no duty to increase the total. Rather he will have a duty to increase the satisfactions of all individuals who exist and possibly all who will exist. Love that is wise will prefer a given number of better satisfied individuals rather than a greater number of less satisfied ones, even if the net total in the universe would be increased by having the greater number of less satisfied ones.

However there is this much truth in utilitarianism: if the numbers are kept the same, an equal love for all the members of a group, or an equal concern for all on the score of selfish need and prudence, or both of these, will give an individual the duty, from his own point of view, of seeking the greatest pleasure for the greatest number of individuals in that group. And that group may be all mankind, or it may be all conscious organisms.

CHAPTER XII

Spiritual Freedom and the Inexorable
Laws of Natural Causation

I—The importance of freedom

THE experience of freedom is inherently satisfactory. It is intrinsic good. Freedom is successful voluntary action. It is the fulfillment of desire. Desire is the spiritual essence of man. The good life and the life with a high degree of freedom are the same thing. Man's highest freedom is his highest good. It is the maximum fulfillment of his spiritual nature, that is, of his desires, and chiefly his major desires or interests. Slavishness is the defeat of desire. The experience of slavishness is intrinsic evil or suffering. There is always some of it in life. Life is bad so far as it is frustrated by internal conflicts or external obstacles. It is good so far as it is unhindered by these,—that is, so far as it is free.

Men's preferences and choices determine in very large measure their long range happiness. In every person's life two alluring and incompatible alternatives are at times presented, one of which would lead to ultimate disaster and the other to genuine spiritual triumph. At such moments it is supremely important that the person in question shall be free to choose, in accordance with reason and foresight, that course which will lead on to creative achievement and long range freedom, in preference to the delusive lures of the disastrous alternative.

Moral responsibility is a fact of human experience, and freedom is absolutely necessary for its existence. A rational person is responsible or answerable, for reward and punishment, to many people, including himself, for his voluntary acts,—but only because he has free-will.

Societies are instrumentally good so far as they nurture and support human freedom. The slavery of ancient Babylonia, Egypt, Greece, and Rome, are a reproach to those civilizations. The political, intellectual, and other freedoms which Greece developed, though they were reared upon the foundation of slavery, are nevertheless her crowning glory. The revival of these freedoms and the addition of some new ones in modern times, after the political and spiritual dictatorships of the Roman Empire and of the Middle Ages, are a precious cultural heritage of contemporary man which he must preserve even if this requires great sacrifice.

II—*The apparent conflict of determinism with freedom*

All this may seem obvious; but another principle, equally clear and true, has seemed to many thinkers to prove that freedom does not exist. This other principle is the uniformity of nature, which comprises two facts, (1) that every event is caused naturally and (2) that the laws of natural causation do not change. Neither the law of gravity nor that of specific gravity nor Boyle's law nor Charles' law nor the law that action and reaction are equal nor the Bernoulli principle, have ever changed one iota. Einstein may have shown that Newton's formulation of the law of gravity was not wholly adequate or accurate. The human expression of the law may be changed. But the actual events which occur in nature follow uniformities that are wholly uniform, and these are the real law.

Another name for the uniformity of nature is determinism. Often it is thought that this is contrary to free-will. If every choice and every voluntary action issuing from a choice are completely determined or caused to be exactly what they are by antecedent conditions, by heredity and environment, then there was never any possibility of their being different from what they are. Then is not the very notion of choice and freedom denied? If a man, X, does A voluntarily in preference to an apparent alternative B, he may think he is choosing A. But if there was no possibility of taking B, is it really a choice? Perhaps there never are any real alternatives. A was pre-determined by or in past causes. The whole future is now pre-determined by present causes. Nobody, it seems, has any real choice. Each one has to follow the course laid out for him.

Then what incentive is there to strive after righteousness or social improvement? The whole future is now unalterably fixed no matter what anybody does. Also there would seem to be no justice in holding anyone responsible for anything he did. No one could possibly have done anything else. Then does not determinism destroy both moral effort and moral responsibility? Then would we not be most unfortunate if it were true? Ought not this doctrine to be suppressed?

But it seems really to be true! So we need to analyse the concepts both of freedom and of determinism very carefully. I shall maintain both that determinism is true and that man's spiritual freedom, creativity, and responsibility are real. The truth is that there is no contradiction between these two principles of determinism and free-will. There has seemed to be one because the concepts of freedom and of causation have not been clearly and properly defined. Each of these has been used popularly in several senses; and there has been much confusion of one sense with another. Our task should now be to define them properly and then to use them in the way in which we have defined them. Their proper definition will be the one by which we shall be helped the most in understanding the matter in hand, namely, the problem of how freedom is possible in a universe of inexorable natural law. Also each definition adopted will be more likely to be helpful if it actually is one of the popular meanings or else is very close to one of them.

Incisive thinkers in nearly every field come up against this problem and almost uniformly bungle it because they are not clear as to exactly what they mean either by freedom or causation. In the last chapter of *War and Peace* the novelist Tolstoy assumes that if the will is caused it cannot be free. In *Civilization on Trial* (Oxford Press, 1948, pp. 31-41) the historian Arnold Toynbee assumes that repetitive historical events are caused and therefore unfree, while nonrepetitive ones are uncaused and free. In *The Nature of the Physical World* (pp. 306-314) A. S. Eddington argues that free-will depends upon indeterminism in the electrons of the brain. Epicurus, about 300 B.C., said that, in order for men to be free, brain atoms would have to swerve from the course prescribed by the laws of natural causation. Many theologians have said that since men have free-will, therefore the supreme being has not caused their sinful acts and is not responsible for these.

A thorough grasp of the basic scientific truth that nature

is uniform, of the precious spiritual principle of human freedom, and of the complete coherence of these two principles both with each other and with all experience, seem to me supremely important for an understanding of the ultimate problems of human life and of its status in the universe.

III—*The truth of determinism*

That determinism is true cannot be proved with absolute certainty. Moreover, contrary to Immanuel Kant, it is very easy to conceive of something as happening without a cause or as being produced by causes such as have other kinds of effects at other times and places. People underestimate their own powers if they think that they are unable to conceive of this. The human mind can conceive of some of the most astonishing and sensational things. Conceiving of things is different from believing that they actually happen. It is barely possible, so far as I know, that something might happen sometime without a cause. But people who have understood the significance of modern science, and who have not been confused by wrong ideas about the free-will problem, are mostly convinced, as I am, that everything really is caused and that the laws are uniform. In other words, determinism is true even if it lacks absolute rational certainty.[1]

A widely publicized defence of indeterminism has come (in 1927) from W. Heisenberg, the German atomic physicist, and A. S. Eddington, the English physicist. Heisenberg has offered evidence indicating that if one could find

---

[1]See my paper "Absolute Truth and the Shadow of Doubt" in *Philosophy of Science*, July 1948, Vol. 15, No. 3, pp. 211 ff.

out the location of an electron one could not discover its velocity, and if one could find out its velocity one could not discover its location. This may be true. But he erroneously inferred from this that if it had a velocity it did not have a location, and that if it had a location it did not have a velocity. Eddington, in his book *The Nature of the Physical World* (pp. 306-314) erroneously inferred from this that causal relations between electronic events were irregular or partly lacking; and from this, as applied to the brain electrons, he erroneously inferred that man's will was in some measure freed from the deadly shackles of materialistic causation.[2]

We should note that in all three kinds of determinism are involved here. (1) There is a *cognitive determinism*. Man can at times determine, find out, or *know* what is going on. Cognitive indeterminacy is doubt or ignorance. Perhaps one cannot determine or know both where an electron is and how fast it is travelling. (2) The *determinism of being* means that a thing has absolutely precise characteristics, whether anybody knows what they are or not. An electron would have indeterminate being if it did not have any exact velocity or location. This is hard to grasp, but I am not prepared to dogmatize about its utter impossibility. I just do not think that it happens. It is interesting that Professor W. P. Montague bases his belief in free-will on an indeterminacy of being, here an indeterminacy in the degree of effort at the moment of action (*Humanist*, January, 1949, Vol. No. 4; p. 184).

It should be clear that cognitive indeterminism does not imply any indeterminism of being. Our not being able to

---

[2]Later studies by Heisenberg and others have indicated that electrons may be waves, and are perhaps quite different from anything man has imagined.

find out where an electron is, is not very good evidence against its being anywhere. Heisenberg's and Eddington's inference as to indeterminism of being from cognitive indeterminism is fallacious.

(3) The causal determinism which we have discussed at some length is what the word 'determinism' usually means when used without any qualifier. It should be clear that proofs of cognitive indeterminism in no way indicate the truth of causal indeterminism. Things can always be caused even if we cannot always find out what the causes are.

In spite of the speculations of the philosophical physicists I think that we are warranted by rational evidence in believing that determinism applies throughout nature without exception. It applies to voluntary actions and to biological and social influences upon these. It applies to all psychological and social phenomena. Both psychology and sociology are sciences. They deal with natural events. An act of will is not a super-natural or a disorderly occurrence. It is a natural link in the causal nexus of the universe. A free will is a successful participation in natural causation, not an escape therefrom. An individual's will expresses his character, which is produced by his past experience, his heredity, and his environment, all of which are, directly or indirectly, produced or created by the supreme being, ultimately reality, or metaphysical absolute,—probably structured energy.

IV—The nature of choice

The causation of will does not make it unfree. The only things that can make it unfree are obstacles which defeat it. If these have causes, as I think they always have, then the will is defeated indirectly by these causes. But if there are

154

no obstacles, the will is undefeated and free, even though caused. Thus causation is intrinsically irrelevant to freedom. A successful will is free whether it is caused or not. A defeated will is unfree whether it is caused or not, and whether the obstructions which defeat it are caused or not. Actually all free wills are caused and all unfreedom is caused. Everything is caused. The issue of freedom vs. unfreedom or slavishness is that of victory vs. defeat, not that of causation vs. non-causation.

The correct definition of freedom is voluntary action. We may if we like add that it is *successful* voluntary action. This however is redundant. If the act occurs it succeeds in occurring. So far as it is defeated, it does not occur. Slavishness is correctly defined as the defeat of an attempt to act voluntarily or of a desire to do so. We may speak of it popularly and loosely as a defeated or thwarted or obstructed voluntary action, if we will remember that, strictly speaking, so far as it is defeated, it is no voluntary action at all. Also, freedom is equivalently defined as the fulfillment of desire and slavishness or unfreedom as its frustration.

Whenever a man, X, performs a voluntary act, A, there are always one or more alternatives that he could have performed instead if he had preferred to. Usually he is aware of certain of these alternatives, and usually he desires in some measure to do them. But even if he is not aware of them, *there is always at least one possible alternative* to A, namely, not to do A and perhaps to make no deliberate effort to do anything else of a positive nature.

The typical situation is where X has the power to do either A or B, and where he prefers A and does it. My thesis is that here he is free even though every element in the situation is caused. He is free because he acts voluntarily. He

155

succeeds in doing A, which is what he wants to do. Only an obstacle preventing him from doing A could make him unfree in this situation. The causes of his preferring A and of his having the power to do A and of his doing A do not prevent him from having what his spirit craves. Rather they make him triumphant. Far from destroying his freedom, they create it. There simply is no contradiction whatever between the inexorable causation of will and its freedom or success. All human freedom is shot through completely with causal compulsion.

But X wants to do B and natural causation prevents. Then X is not free as to B. His desire to do B is defeated by the stronger conflicting desire to do A. A and B being alternatives, he cannot do both. He has more freedom, at least for the moment, in doing A than unfreedom in not doing B. But in a choice where there is any desire at all for the rejected alternative, there is some unfreedom.

Thus, due to the causal determination of his will by heredity and environment, *X could not do B*. He had to do what he did. All people have to do what they do. This fact makes some people think that it is a mistake to believe in real or objective choice. But it is no mistake. Objective choice is what the word 'choice' means in English, and X actually did what 'choice' means; we are all doing it all the time while we are alive and awake. X had two alternatives, A and B, either of which he had the power to do if he preferred. He preferred A over B. He chose A rather than B. He did A. *He could have done B* if he had preferred B. This whole situation contains what 'choice' means in the English language. X really chose A.

But note that while he could have done B if he had preferred, he could have done it *only* if he had preferred; and

156

he did not prefer. So *he could not have done B.* The causes of his preferring A over B prevented him from doing B. Causal determinism made the doing of B impossible for him. The single line of the causal sequence of events was fixed irrevocably by past causes and by the laws of nature, and no deviation was possible. But still X had a real objective choice; and he could have done B if he had preferred B. Of course he could not have preferred B, due to the causes of his preference for A. But he did not want to prefer B, so there was no unfreedom in not being able to. There is no unfreedom in not being able to do what he does not want to do. He wanted to prefer A, not B. Anybody can prefer anything he likes. Of course his liking will be caused by heredity and environment. Also X wanted to *do* B, but he was prevented. There he was unfree. But his choice was genuine and free, as every choice must be, in that he chose and did what he preferred to do, and that he could have performed an alternative if he had preferred. I have said both that he wanted to *do* B and that he did not want to *prefer* B. This holds. The distinction here between *do* and *prefer* is basic.

X could have done B if he had preferred; but, due to the causal necessity of his not preferring B, *he could not have done B.* Is this a contradiction? Not if two meanings of 'could' are recognized. $Could_1$ includes in its meaning the meaning of the phrase 'if he preferred'. $Could_2$ includes in its meaning the meaning of the phrase 'if or since he did not prefer'. Then X $could_1$ have done B, but he $could_2$ not have done B. Obviously there is no contradiction.

To summarize, X is free to do A and unfree to do B. He wants to do A and he does it. He wants to do B and he cannot do it. His choice is free. He can choose and do whichever he prefers. But natural causation here rigidly determines every event. Nothing could$_2$ possibly have happened except what did happen.

Hitler could$_2$ not have kept the peace in 1939. The hereditary and environmental factors which made him what he was, also made peace causally impossible. He was caused to prefer war and to have the power to make war. That made war inevitable. He had free-will, of course. He made war voluntarily, and he could$_1$ have kept the peace *if he had preferred*. He acted as a responsible agent, and he was held responsible. But he could$_1$ have kept the peace *only if he had preferred* to keep it. He did not prefer to keep it, so he could$_2$ not do so. He had to do what he actually preferred. Nobody can ever do voluntarily anything except what he prefers, among the possible alternatives.

V—The impossibility of doing what one does not prefer

This last is an important principle. A man may prefer something which he has not the power to do, and then he will not do it because he cannot. But among the possible alternatives, by which I mean the ones he can do if he prefers, he always does the one which he actually prefers, that is, the one for which he has the strongest desire. He is compelled by natural causation to do this freely and voluntarily. Suppose he is in a room and prefers to stay there but is ordered to leave by four rough persons who threaten him with violence unless he moves out. He goes out through fear, even though he may say that he prefers to stay. But actually he does not prefer to stay. He prefers going out and not suffering violence, rather than staying in and being beaten. He does voluntarily what he prefers among those alternatives which he has the power to do. He must do this at all times when he is alive and awake.

Again suppose that he prefers to defy the four rough persons, and that they seize him by his arms and legs and throw him out the door. Has he not done what he did not prefer? He has not done it voluntarily. His body has gone through the motions of leaving the room, but his soul has not willed it. The rule is that no one can do voluntarily anything which he does not prefer. But superior external forces can put him through various motions against his will. Really his going forth is an act of the four rough persons, not of his. But if, as he travels out through the door, he prefers to struggle against the inevitable, he is free to struggle. In case he prefers to relax and let fate take its course unopposed, he is free to do that. Whichever of these alternatives he prefers he will have to do freely. He cannot voluntarily do anything except what he prefers, among the alternatives which he has the strength to do.

VI—The degrees of human freedom

This raises the problem of the degrees of human freedom. Everyone is free in some degree as long as he is alive and awake. Freedom belongs to the very essence of the human spirit. But also everyone is almost always partly slavish. X was unfree in not being able to do B, which he desired to do; and there is a B in nearly every such situation. Man is a frustrated animal. Every soul is part free and part slave. We call a man slavish when slavishness predominates. The man who leaves the room through fear is being slavish. The man who is thrown out the door is still more slavish. Also each is slightly free. Each is doing successfully what he prefers among the alternatives that he has the strength to do. But for each there is something else that he has not the strength to do, and that he prefers very much more. A man has little freedom if he cannot do the things he desires very much to do. If a person is bound hand and foot and gagged and locked in a dungeon cell, he still would probably be able and free either to struggle, or not, as he preferred. If he were too sick and weak to struggle he would be free either to think about struggling or about something else. He is free while he is alive and awake. But here he is not very free.

There is a sense in which stone walls do not a prison make, nor iron bars a cage. If a man could keep out of jail only by doing what would make him lose his self-respect, then his being in jail with his self-respect means more freedom and less frustration for him than if he were outside.

The highest degree of freedom would be the situation where in every moment at least one alternative was open which was most deeply satisfying to the individual involved. This is an ideal to which we can only approximate here below. But 'the more freedom the better' is a basic principle which is clearly equivalent to the principle that 'the more satisfaction in the long run the better'.

VII—Freedom of preference

One interesting attack upon the whole notion of causal freedom focuses on the preference which initiates the voluntary act. X's freedom seems to consist in the fact that he does A by preference and that he could have done B if he had preferred. But could he have preferred? Heredity and environment saw to it that he did not prefer B. Apparently there was no possibility of his preferring B. If freedom is excluded here in the preference which lies at the source of the voluntary act, perhaps the supposed freedom in the act itself, which I have been describing and praising, may be illusory.

But, remembering that freedom is a successful voluntary action, it is not excluded here. X is free to prefer anything he likes. Preferring is desiring one alternative more than another. X can desire anything he wishes to desire. And he can desire any one thing more than anything else, if he wishes to do so. His liking or wishing will always be caused by heredity and environment, but he still is free to desire and to prefer anything he likes. Liking to desire or to prefer anything is obviously the same as desiring or preferring it.

Clearly, the term 'freedom' is applicable only to a situation in which there already exists an actual desire and preference. How these came into existence, whether by causes or not, is irrelevant to the question of whether they are free.

Wishing, desiring, and preferring are really forms of voluntary action. They are actions which take place within the mind. They are obviously all caused; and, like all voluntary actions, they are free when successful. They are always successful. One always succeeds in desiring or preferring what he wants to desire or to prefer.

VIII—The determinism of logical necessity or formal causation

We have seen that all freedom is completely permeated with causal necessity. It is also completely permeated with logical necessity. Logic is the meanings of our words. While we stick to our meanings we are bound by them. If we do not stick to them our thinking becomes untrustworthy. It is by causal necessity that heredity and environment *make* freedom in a process which Aristotle called '*efficient* causation' and which today scientists call just 'causation' without any qualifier. It is by logical necessity that preference plus power *make* freedom in a process which Aristotle called '*formal* causation.' Preference and power are characteristics, qualities, or forms which, taken together, contain the quality of freedom. Where they are, it must necessarily be, whether it is caused by heredity and environment or not. If X has the preference and the power to do A he must do it freely by logical necessity. There is not the slightest possibility of his not doing it. What could prevent? If an external obstacle stopped him he would not have the power. But we are supposing that he has the power. If an opposed and stronger desire in his own mind, say for C, inhibited his doing A, then he would prefer C, not A. But we are supposing that he prefers A.

Also X's unfreedom to do B, when he prefers A, an alternative, is logically necessary. It flows from the meanings of 'alternative' and 'preference.' Alternatives are things which cannot both be done. A preference is a stronger desire for one alternative than for another. X cannot desire A more than he desires B at the same time he desires B more than he desires A. It is logically impossible for him to prefer B if he prefers A. Moreover, it is logically impossible for X to do anything voluntarily unless he prefers it among all of the possible alternatives. Therefore, by logic, he is not free or able to do B.

IX—The uselessness of indeterminism

All of this holds true entirely apart from natural causation. It holds if we use our words consistently in their proper meanings, that is, in those traditional meanings which best facilitate our understanding of the problem. If preference plus power are present, there is freedom even if both are wholly caused in accordance with inexorable natural law. And where either preference or power or both are absent, there freedom is absent, even if the situation is uncaused. Suppose that just prior to X's preference for A over B there were a gap in the causal sequences in his mind. Suppose that either his preference for A or his power to do A, or both, were uncaused. Clearly that fact would not increase his freedom in the slightest degree. It would not help him to do A successfully. He can do this anyhow. It would not enable him to prefer B, or to do B, if he preferred A.

Perhaps it would enable him to prefer B and not prefer A any more. But the ability to do this would not be freedom unless he wanted to prefer B rather than A. And if he wanted to prefer B rather than A in a completely deterministic system he would be able to do so. We have seen that X can prefer anything he wants to, even when his wanting to, that is, even when his preferring it, is absolutely caused by heredity and environment.

The same holds if X's preference or power were only partly caused, or if they were, perhaps, wholly caused in accordance with variable natural laws so that a given kind of cause sometimes produced one kind of preference and sometimes another under similar circumstances. X would have no more freedom if this were the actual case than he would under rigid determinism. Thus not only is indeterminism false, but also it would be of no use to anybody if it were true.

CHAPTER XIII

Some Prevalent Errors about Freedom and Causation

I—The soul as a visitor from another world

THE prevalence of the notion that complete natural causation in psychological events would annul all human freedom is probably due in part to the old belief, frequently expressed by Platonists and other mystics, that the human soul is a transient alien here below, a visitor from a higher sphere, a pure spiritual essence caught in the prison house of the flesh but ever yearning to escape and to return to its more congenial native habitat.[1] If this were so, probably any natural biological causal influences, or social influences from other organisms, would tend to divert it from its high destiny as determined by its super-natural origin and its transcendent ethereal nature. Thus all natural causation would be an obstacle to the fulfillment of its deepest aspirations, and would produce unfreedom.

Also, if this were so, the soul would be completely engulfed in a super-natural or transcendent determinism which mystics and theologians have seldom recognized.

---

[1]For a typical expression of this idea see *Philosophical Writings of Philo*; edited by Hans Lewy; Phaidon Press, Oxford; 1946, pp. 36-37. ". . . the wise . . . are counted as aliens and sojourners." ". . . the heavenly region . . . is their native land; the earthly region . . . is a foreign country." "Each of us has come into this world as into a foreign city, in which before our birth we had no part."
Philo was a Jewish philosopher who was deeply influenced by Plato. He lived in Alexandria about the time of Jesus.

I believe that the idea of the soul as an alien here below is influential in the backs of the minds of many contemporary thinkers. A whole-hearted and thorough-going naturalism is indispensable for a just appreciation of these matters. The human soul or personality is an emergent product of two natural evolutionary processes, namely, biological and cultural evolution.

II—*The supposed slavishness involved in natural causation*

One misunderstanding of causation which drives some people into the indeterministic fold is the notion that effects are always ignominiously subservient to their causes and to the laws of their causation.

First, as to causes, slaves are often humiliated by being caused or compelled to do what their masters command. Their behavior is free only in a very low degree, because it is the effect of the causal influence of the master. But this fact does not indicate that all effects are the slaves of their causes. It is just that the commands of slave-owners do happen to obstruct the slaves' deepest desires. Successful men are not humiliated or enslaved when they are caused by heredity and environment to succeed and perhaps to know that they are thus being caused to succeed. The causes of success make freedom. Only obstacles and the causes of obstacles make slavishness.

Some think that subjection to natural law is in itself slavish. This is perhaps partly due to the analogy between natural laws and legislative statutes. People are denied a certain freedom when they live under political laws. They are often menaced with dire punishment if they violate the edicts of the state. However, man's highest freedom is impossible apart from the state and its laws. Also, neither his highest freedom, nor any freedom, ever occur without causation according to the laws of nature.

Moreover, these laws involve no threats of punishment for infractions. They cannot be violated. Everything takes place in accordance with them. They are simply the causally necessary sequences which do in fact occur in the natural course of events.

Sometimes their operation involves frustration and slavishness. But rational human beings will not seek to cure this by violating or abrogating natural law. Rather they will seek to produce causes which, operating still in accordance with natural law, will remove the frustrations and produce freedom.

III—*The container theory of causation*

Another misconception of causation is the theory that it operates like the emptying of a container. William James has popularized this theory in recent years. He said that if determinism were true, then nothing new could ever happen. He assumed that effects were always originally contained in their causes and literally came out of these in the process of causation. If this were so it would follow that any truly novel event would have to occur uncaused. Determinism, said James, would make this a 'block' universe in which everything would be fixed and rigid and determinate and determined. His ardent spirit shuddered at the thought. He was vividly aware of evolution and progress. He knew that genuine novelty was constantly occurring. He felt a great spontaneity and creativity within himself. He proclaimed that the universe was 'open.' Man is capable of free creative choices which break the shackling chains or laws of container causation.

One form that this container theory has taken is that causal relations are, or are like, rational, logical, and mathematical relations. Some metaphysical rationalists, like Descartes and Spinoza in the seventeenth century, have believed that the whole universe operated strictly according to rational principles, which, in their application to physical-spatial things, were essentially mathematical. Analytical geometry and calculus express shapes and motions by equations.

In mathematics, two things plus three other things *make* five things because 'two things plus three other things' *contain* 'five things.' Also, in geometry, the definitions, axioms, and postulates produce or create all of the theorems because they contain within them the logical and mathematical essences of all the theorems. And the premises of a syllogism imply the conclusion because they contain it. It is drawn out of them by a process of dialectical or logical analysis. Their truth 'makes' the conclusion true by logic or reason. Then, applying these principles to the processes of nature, Descartes and Spinoza believed that all natural effects were derived from causes, which already contain them, by a process of dialectical or mathematical implication and deduction. The necessity of natural causation is mathematical or logical necessity. And the knowledge of effects from their causes is a matter of the dialectical elucidation of the nature of the causes.

This logico-mathematical or container theory of causation was refuted by the Scotchman David Hume in 1739.[2]

---

[2] *A Treatise of Human Nature.*

Hume showed that causation is not logically necessary. He said that it is just uniform succession. Until you find out by experience, you do not know what effect will follow from any given cause. Merely examining a cause does not reveal what the effect will be, because the effect is not tucked away inside the cause. The effect may be almost utterly different from the cause. The effect, said Hume, is merely what always succeeds the cause. It may be brand new.

I think that Hume was largely right. Effects can be brand new in some respects. True, they appear never to have any more energy in them than was in their causes. Container causation probably holds true as to energy. But effects can and often do have much more value than their causes, and they often have new emergent qualities and properties never seen or heard of before. In both biological and cultural evolution, brand new things have been caused millions of times. Every step in biological evolution was caused and was novel. Probably nothing like reptiles had ever existed in the whole universe before those beasts evolved from amphibians in the Paleozoic Age; and yet there were causes of this new departure in evolution,—causes which did not contain their effects.

Also when men evolved beyond the level of apes, their like probably had not existed in earlier ages; but there were doubtless causes of their inception. Moreover, every step in cultural evolution has been voluntary and free and novel,—and has been caused. When the Athenians invented a democratic constitution for their city state in 509 B.C. they were being original and they were acting freely and voluntarily. And yet there were causes of their inventing democracy at that particular juncture in human affairs. And when some men in western Europe in modern times began to perfect laboratory techniques for scientific research, their action was free, voluntary, and original, and was caused by complex social, psychological, and biological forces.

Hume failed to guard sufficiently against the fallacy of *post hoc ergo propter hoc*.[3] Causation is not mere uniform succession. It is a special kind of succession in which, in the absence of any obstructing factor, you cannot have the antecedent without getting the consequent. Day and night succeed each other uniformly, but they do not cause each other. It is easy to see that under certain easily imaginable though astronomically sensational circumstances, either day or night might occur without being followed by the other. Therefore neither is the cause of the other. But when sequences would stay uniform no matter how the situation were varied, we infer that there is a necessary causal link between antecedent and consequent.

Natural causal necessity is a unique kind of necessity. It is not mathematical, logical, rational, or moral necessity, or anything else except natural causal necessity. It cannot be explained by analysis into any other principle. It is thus indefinable. But it can be pointed at. It is a unique and universal aspect of the ultimate nature of things. Approximate synonyms of it are 'making' and 'producing'. All languages have words for this unique process of efficient causing, because all people have the idea, which is derived from their experience.

The erroneous notion that ordinary efficient causation is mathematical or logical or rational is explainable historically. It has appeared twice in the earlier stages of great cultural developments, in ancient Greece and in modern times, when mathematics was the intellectual discipline of

---

[3]After this and therefore because of this.

dominating interest and the chief growing point of man's scientific culture. Especially in such periods, enlightened men tend to interpret the whole universe in terms of the science which seems most important to them and which they know best.

IV—Indirect causation

Another misinterpretation of causation is the one which assumes that if, for instance, men are caused or made to live partly virtuous and partly sinful lives by an heredity and an environment which are, themselves, produced by the supreme being or ultimate reality, then really the only thing that causes men's virtues and vices is the supreme being. If A causes B, B causes C, and C causes D, it is supposed that C does not really cause D. But of course the truth is that A and B each causes D more or less indirectly, and C causes it directly. The supreme being is omnipotent in the sense that it does everything that is done. But it does a lot of things indirectly, and its omnipotence is no denial that men's own natures cause their own acts, including all their virtues and vices, directly. Then, as we shall see in the next chapter, if and so far as men are rational and act voluntarily, they are morally responsible both for their virtues and for their vices. And if, and so far as, the supreme being is rational and acts voluntarily in causing (mostly indirectly) men's virtues and vices, it too is morally responsible for these.

Consider the case of the successive generations of men. A grandson is indirectly produced by his four grandparents and is directly produced by his two parents. Everything he does is partly an effect of events in the lives of these six people. It is also partly caused by many other factors in his environment. And still the grandson himself does whatever he does, and is morally responsible for it, if he acts rationally and voluntarily. His ancestors are also morally responsible for his virtues and for his vices, so far as they were rational and so far as what they did was an intentional or negligent cause of his behavior.

V—*Consciousness and causation*

Another error leading to mistakes about free-will is the notion of consciousness as something which miraculously transcends causation. The status of consciousness in nature is a baffling subject. The human mind cannot grasp it fully. But I think we can understand something about it. Consciousness is a product of two natural causal evolutionary processes, namely, biological and cultural evolution. It is probably not a force. As Santayana has indicated, it appears to be rather the light of the mind than the driving power. The power is the biological energy in the neurones. Consciousness is an emergent quality or aspect of the central nervous system. Its relation to the system is approximately that of an attribute to a substance. It is present during most intelligent behavior. Sometimes a man will do intelligent things of which he is hardly conscious at the time. And a good many of the mental processes involved in reasoning and willing are subconscious. But probably consciousness necessarily occurs at some stage in all intelligent voluntary conduct. Consciousness is a necessary aspect of an enlightened will.

However, it seems unlikely that consciousness can transmit any energy. Consider its analogy to the cylindricality of a piston in a cylinder of a gasoline engine. Cylindricality, in the correct diameter, is an abstract emergent property of the metal. Separate particles of the iron do not have it. But the whole metal part does have it. This form is necessary in order that the piston shall fit snugly into the surrounding metal of the cylinder and yet slide freely up and down, and thus this form is an indispensable factor in the transmission of energy from the burning hydro-carbons in the cylinder head to the crank shaft. Piston and cylinder must fit each other with very narrow tolerances, or else the energy will not be transmitted. But the abstract quality of cylindricality itself transmits no energy. And similarly, consciousness is an indispensable element in the intelligent action of a human organism, even though, as an abstract emergent property of the nervous system, it probably transmits no actual energy itself. It is, as we noted above, the light of the mind, not the driving force. It is the foam on the crest of the wave. There is no push in it.

The human mind should be regarded as comprising both consciousness and the nervous system. An idea has a conscious aspect and a neurological aspect. Also the rational will has these two aspects. All its energy is located in the latter. Because of the latter, ideas and volitions are efficacious. Man, by his ideas and will, has built a vast cultural heritage in the last million years which has transformed his life. Ideas and a lot of good will, and some bad will, are today working further transformations. But in all these transformations it is the energy in the neurones that supplies the drive. The rational will is basically a neurological force. Psychological energy is a refinement of physical and biological energy. Every act of will is caused by the nervous system of the organism, and, indirectly, by past influences upon that system. These influences are hereditary and environmental, and can mostly be traced back to biological and cultural evolution. The two evolutions, and all other influences, are due, in the last analysis, to the ultimate nature of things, or the supreme being.

VI—Chance and probability

Some have rejected determinism on the ground that if it were true all chance and uncertainty, especially as to the future, would be purely subjective. These things, it is said, would be due merely to human ignorance. The truth is that determinism does imply the subjectivity of chance, but this is no argument against determinism. Chance is in fact subjective. Chance or probability is the strength of the evidence that a person has indicating that some proposition is true. This is a large subject and I have treated it at some length elsewhere.[4] Here let me sketch the basic principles.

The word 'chance' may of course be used in an objective sense to mean indeterminism. But since there is no such thing it would be better not to use it in this meaning. Also this is not the more ordinary usage. Ordinarily speaking, if I meet a friend down town by chance, that means that we did not know definitely about the meeting ahead of time. If we planned it, then it was not chance. Things which are done intentionally and with foreknowledge are not chance from the points of view of those who have the knowledge. But even if my friend and I did not expect to see each other, still there were causes of our meeting. It was a matter of timing. The causes timed the occurrence absolutely. Indeterminism is not needed to account for our actual expe-

---

[4]*Philosophy of Science*, July 1948, Vol. 15, No. 3.

riences of chance and accident. In chance meetings there was insufficient probability or evidence in someone's mind ahead of time as to what was going to happen. His knowledge was lacking or incomplete. A basic principle of the theory of probability is that chances vary with the strength or probative efficacy of the evidence. If a person knows that a normally shaped coin is to be flipped and that one side of it is heads, then the strength or probative efficacy of the evidence, indicating to him that heads will come, is about 50%. That is, the chance of getting heads is about 1/2. The state of the evidence in his mind before the throw is what is called the 'base.' This chance or probability is no denial of the universal efficacy of absolute invariable causal law in determining every detail of the motion of the coin and thus in determining which side comes up.

Probability can also mean the actual recurrences of a chance or imperfectly understood phenomenon, such as the number of times that heads comes up in a given number of flips. This might be called 'recurrence probability' to distinguish it from the first meaning, which might be called 'evidential probability,' subjective probability, ordinary probability, or just probability.[5] Recurrences would of course themselves be evidential, but there are other evidences too, such as one's knowledge of the shape of the coin, one's knowledge that it is not likely to split through the middle and fall with both of the original sides down, and also all of the evidence one has indicating that the laws of nature will not suddenly change in such manner as to affect the outcome.

---

[5]See my paper on this subject in *Philosophical Review*, Vol. 47, No. 4, 414 ff., July 1938. Also see *Phil Rev.*, Vol. 48, No. 6, pp. 632 ff., Nov. 1939.

VII—Can men alter the future?

Some make the mistake of thinking that if the future is all predetermined then human effort is futile. Actually the future is unalterable, but still man can probably make further progress by exerting his will, courage, and intelligence.

It is fundamental that the past cannot be made different from exactly what it was, that the present cannot be made different from exactly what it is, and that the future can never be made different from exactly what it will be. This is due essentially or formally (in Aristotelian terminology) to the determinism of being, and only efficiently, not essentially, to ordinary causal determinism. The latter, has, of course, in fact made everything just what it is at the time that it is it. But even if everything were partly or wholly uncaused, still past, present, and future could never be different from exactly what they were, are, and will be.

All past crimes and all past social injustice have been 100% causally inevitable. The criminals could have acted virtuously if they had preferred, but heredity and environment caused them not to prefer. The people who voluntarily set up social laws, customs, and institutions, involving social injustice, could have set up other laws etc., if they had preferred to,—laws etc., which would have involved other forms of social injustice and perhaps much less of it. But heredity and environment caused them to prefer to set up just the laws etc. they did, among those which they had the power to establish. In the same sense all present and future crime and injustice are and will be 100% causally inevitable. This may make it look futile to attempt to prevent criminal violation of just laws and to renovate unjust ones. We are not permitted to break the laws of natural causation in order to enforce or to reform our man-made laws.

Still, moral and social reform is not really futile. When the causes of crime are, in accordance with the inexorable laws of nature, caused to be removed, the non-occurrence of crime will be just as causally inevitable as all the crimes of history have been. When the causes of social justice are caused to occur, social justice will be equally inevitable. It is a matter of education and wise social leadership, and possibly a bit of negative eugenics to wipe out some of the bad hereditary strains. This education and leadership and eugenics will not occur unless they are caused. But in part they have been caused already. Probably they will be caused to exist and to operate more effectively as biological and cultural evolution continue on their respective ways.

Also efforts to understand this problem should help a little. These efforts will not occur unless they are caused. But already some have been caused. And I believe that in the future better efforts giving a deeper understanding of the subject will be caused.

It is important to realize that while man can never make the future different from what it will be, still there are three important things that he can do which have been confused with changing the future. (1) He can often make it different from what somebody thought it would be. People can have false ideas about what is coming. But making a thing different from somebody's false idea of it, is not changing it. (2) Also man can often make the future partly different from what the past has been and what the present is. But again, this is not changing the future. It is creating the future. (3) Finally, the actual exertion of man's will always necessarily makes the future partly different from what it

176

would have been if man had not thus exerted his will. That is, man's will is causally efficacious. Every efficacious or efficient cause, every falling raindrop, every motion of the planet Neptune, makes the future different from what it would have been if that cause had not operated. And man's will is triumphant and free so far as it creates a future that he desires, prefers, and enjoys.

VIII—Foreknowledge and happiness

It is very unlikely that any man will ever be able to foresee the entire future, or any considerable part of it, with either a high degree of accuracy or a high degree of probability. We know something about things to come, but we do not know much. In general, the more a man knows about the future the better. Foreknowledge helps one to control his own destiny wisely; that is, in part it *causes* him to do this. Some may feel that it is better not to know about the calamities which are in store for us. Perhaps if we are destined to die young we will be happier while we live if we do not know about it. However, I believe that the control which knowledge gives is likely to produce more happiness than will be lost through our finding out about impending and inevitable disaster. And any one who still dreads to look far ahead may be consoled by reflecting on how extremely limited our knowledge is always likely to remain.

IX—The supposition of complete foreknowledge

Some philosophers have been concerned about the relation of human freedom to complete foreknowledge, supposing such knowledge to exist. If any man or deity could foresee

177

the entire future of the whole universe in all detail, would that make human freedom impossible? Suppose that a being with complete prevision predicted a specific voluntary act of a particular man on a certain date ten years hence. Then if, when the date came around, the man preferred not to perform that act, one might ask, would he have to do it against his will? If so, he certainly would not be free. Would complete foreknowledge negate freedom?

Really it would not. If the man was not going to prefer that act on that date, perfect foreknowledge would have predicted that he would not. To know that a man will do something voluntarily at a definite time is to know that he will have the preference and the power to do it at that time. In case this is known truly, he will in fact prefer that act and do it voluntarily and freely on that day. Should he lack either preference or power, then an earlier belief that he would voluntarily do that act on that day would not be knowledge. A false belief is not knowledge.

We should note that if a man had a complete knowledge of the present situation in the universe and of the laws of its causal operations, his ability to foretell any event in the future would not necessarily follow, La Place to the contrary notwithstanding. The person who had this complete knowledge of laws and of present facts would not be able to foretell the nature of any new emergent qualities, such as, for instance, new colors not yet experienced and not just combinations of old colors, which were actually going to emerge in the future course of biological evolution.

However, a transcendent deity whose mind could grasp all past, present, and future times in one synthetic insight, would probably be able to predict anything at all that was going to happen, even if it were to be uncaused.

X—Fatalism

Finally let me point out that the natural determinism which I have defended in this chapter is quite different from what is usually called fatalism. Fatalism means that *no matter what a man chooses and does,* an event that was decreed by fate, or by some spirit, will necessarily occur. This is the sort of thing we run into in the *Arabian Nights.* My theory is that, largely *because of what a man chooses and does,* future events, which are determined by natural law, will necessarily occur.

Also in fatalism the idea is almost always present that the future event is foreseen by someone. Foresight is not at all implied in the doctrine of determinism.

Chapter XIV

Wrath and moral responsibility

I—The compatibility of determinism with wrath and moral responsibility

THERE is a widespread belief that if determinism were true we should stop holding people responsible both for their sins and for their virtues. The absolute inevitability of their acts might seem to indicate the truth of two revolutionary principles.

(1) Sinners would not be responsible for the evil deeds which they intentionally or negligently committed. It appears irrational to blame and to punish them for what they could not help doing.

(2) A man ought never to be angry at malefactors who have deliberately or negligently injured him. Possibly he should not wreak his vengeance upon people who have damaged him, when their doing it was utterly inevitable.

I shall contend that determinism involves neither of these principles. All choices and all wills are caused by heredity and environment; and also most intentional and negligent malefactors are morally responsible for what they do. They should be punished. Moreover, wrath is sometimes a proper reaction to deliberate or negligent injury.

First let us consider wrath.

II—Wrath

Wrath was developed originally as a survival factor in biological evolution. Certain animals have lived more successfully because they have occasionally become furious at a dangerous enemy who intentionally or negligently injured them. Their fury has tended to make them more successful in disabling him. They could hurt him more when they were enthusiastic about it. Once he was disabled they were safer. He may not have dared to brave their wrath again. If the injury he did was through negligence he was likely to be more careful next time. Or he may have been unable to do any more damage because he was crippled or killed. Through the fury and resentment of his victims his will and desire to injure them, or his lack of will and desire not to injure them, may have been altered; or his ability to injure them may have been reduced.

Thus anger has given some measure of security against the malice and the negligence of others in the primeval forest. It has doubtless saved many of the lives which have been saved in the struggle for existence. The higher types of animal would not now possess it to the degree that they do had it not been an important survival factor. It has done much good in the world. It is, in a measure, justified, because it, and its consequences, have been, in a measure, satisfactory.

To-day its role is similar to the role it has played from the beginning of its evolutionary career. Against anyone who has injured others through what is, from their point of view, a fault in his will, namely, through malice or negligence, resentment is a natural reaction, which is likely on many occasions to implement survival. Moreover, if normal people inhibit it too much, they are not usually able to respect themselves. Few can be perfectly content if they let an intentional insult or injury go by without some vindictive response.

It is, I think, common experience that if the wills, desires, and attitudes of persons who injure a man were not at fault, that is, if those persons were neither malicious nor negligent, he would not normally feel any lust for vengeance. Vengeance is supposed to cure defects in other people's wills and attitudes or to minimize the evil consequences of those defects. If there has been no defect it is silly for a man to lose his temper. A rational person does not normally resent injuries done him by others if the others did not mean to hurt him and were not at all negligent. If they took an attitude of good will and if they used due care, they were not to blame, and his attitude-changing, will-inoculating passion of resentment would be quite out of order.

Thus the question of whether a rational and normal person would be angry at others is not at all the question of whether their wills and desires were caused or not. The important question is Did the injury flow from a will or attitude or desire of theirs which was not friendly enough to him? If it did not he will not resent it. If it did he will feel resentful; and, under these circumstances, he should feel so.

III—*Evils involved in vengeance, and their avoidance*

Some will deny that vengeance is ever right. Saintly moralists have emphasized its drawbacks. We must not close our eyes to the evils it involves. It is dangerous stuff. Vengeance is dynamite. I think that it is sometimes useful; but it needs to be kept under strict control. Man is far too prone to lose his temper and to retaliate. He frequently gets himself into trouble by doing this. Often he tries and fails to disable his enemies, and then they do more damage to him because he tried. Also, when he succeeds in penalizing them, he causes at times such bitterness in their hearts that they bide their time and strike him down later. Surviving victims tend to remember such things as the Maine, the Treaty of Versailles, and Pearl Harbor. And often, by too quick and violent retaliation, a man makes bitter enemies of those who once did only a slight injury to him, and who could, by forgiveness, have been turned into much needed friends. Thus a man may penalize himself seriously by his own excessive irascibility.

Also some men are silly enough to lose their tempers when injured by the unintentional and non-negligent acts of others, or even when injured by inanimate objects. Such behavior is very likely to produce much more grief than it is worth.

Probably there have been saints who have mortified their vindictive tendencies to the point where they could respect themselves without any retaliation, and who have lived long enough and satisfactorily enough to call their lives on the whole intrinsically good. Non-resistance is a possible human attitude. And it may be practical in some cases where spiritual demands have been subjected to hostile and almost invincible force. Jesus, St. Francis, and Gandhi, have gotten some results by it. It is justified so far as it produces a greater satisfaction, in the long run, than any alternative could produce. But it is a slavish virtue, and man does not live slavishly if he can avoid it. Probably very few people will ever find happiness by making it a universal rule of conduct.

Like all products of biological evolution, wrath is roughly and approximately beneficent, though very imperfect in its crude instinctive form. It needs to be refined and re-directed by reason and culture, so as to function harmoniously in a good life without entailing those evil consequences which all too frequently have accompanied it. There is a time for resentment, as there is a time for forgiveness, and either of these passions will be virtuous, if the time and the place and the degree and the person who functions as the object are all right. In order to make all these things right, men need reason and good habits. Vengeance must be subjected to rational control.

One case where vengeance operates beneficently is in the punishment of criminals. Most law-abiding citizens desire that the perpetrator of some particularly shocking crime shall suffer. They are aroused largely by their sympathy for the victim. They experience a genuine lust for vengeance, which is usually satisfied when the law exacts its penalty. Their vindictiveness creates a powerful body of public opinion which tends to keep the law-enforcement officials on the alert, and to make them work efficiently in protecting society by the suppression of crime. The public's vengeful passions are extremely beneficent provided the culprit is given a fair trial, and provided that the penalty imposed is in accordance with the law, and provided that the law is just. Lynching is, of course, the case where these passions perniciously break through the restrictions imposed by law and reason.

In conclusion we should note that life is hard and that there is so much suffering in it that every innocent or beneficent source of satisfaction and enjoyment may properly be cultivated. Rational vengeance is surely one such source.

IV—The nature of moral responsibility

Let us now consider how the objects of public wrath are

in most cases actually culpable and responsible for their misdeeds.

In order that an individual shall be morally responsible for what he does it is not at all necessary that his acts shall be uncaused. It is only necessary that he shall be a rational person and that he shall act voluntarily. Responsibility means answerability. Rational persons are rightly compelled to answer for their voluntary acts.

They answer always either to some one person or to several. Responsibility is always relative to one or more points of view. A man is answerable to society, that is, to the individuals who make up society, or to his employer, or to himself, for what he has done deliberately or carelessly in a lucid moment. Certain individuals and groups demand that he shall give an account of himself, and he must respond to their demand. They hold him responsible. His being responsible, say, to society, means that society will be right, from its points of view, in inquiring into his conduct and in attempting to reward or punish him for what he has done. And it will in fact be right, from its points of view, if rewarding or punishing him will satisfy its interests best in the long run, that is, if these rewards or punishments will satisfy its desires for expressing either gratitude or resentment, and if they will influence his conduct so as to make him more cooperative or less hostile. Moreover, prizes and penalties will thus influence his *voluntary* actions so far as he is *rational*. Responsibility, as we have indicated, implies both volition and rationality. An irrational organism, or one which performed no voluntary behavior at all, would not be influenced in any degree for the better by rewards or punishments, and so would be utterly irresponsible.

Blame attaches to a man only on account of injurious acts

which he has performed voluntarily while he was rational, and only if some person ought, from that person's point of view, to punish him.

V—The responsibility of criminals to society

Society holds a man responsible for the evil he does partly in order to wreak its vengeance upon him. Law-abiding citizens sympathize with the victim of a crime, especially if it is revolting crime and if the victim was pure and innocent. They demand vengeance upon the culprit. They desire that he shall suffer. They are interested in causing him pain. As we have indicated, this interest is beneficent and rational when kept within the bounds set by reason and by just laws. But it is a dangerous passion, and may cause enough suffering to far outweigh the satisfaction which its successful functioning always produces. Also it has led to the silly and expensive practice of curing a sick criminal in order to execute him, when he would die naturally if left alone. But its existence is one of the things that make criminals responsible to society for their crimes. It gives society a genuine satisfaction in punishing criminals, and thus it creates a genuine obligation for society to punish them.

Another motive which leads society to hold individuals morally responsible for their misdeeds is self-defense. Crime threatens the existence of society. Society has a long-range interest in diminishing it or stamping it out. Every enlightened society therefore practices rational and dispassionate self-defense. It puts a criminal in jail partly to restrain him from doing any damage. Also it executes a particularly dangerous criminal, partly in order to render him incapable of further crime. It also hopes and intends that by these penal-

186

ties other persons who contemplate crime will be deterred. And society also hopes and intends that the culprit himself, if he is released after a term in jail, will be deterred from further malefaction. These hopes are only partly realized. A man's experiences in jail, and the suspicious attitude of normal citizens toward him after his release, often counteract the deterrent effect of his incarceration upon his antisocial propensities. Nevertheless incarceration does *tend* to prevent criminals from repeating their offences, so far as they are rational, even if other forces more than counterbalance this tendency. Also, while actual criminals are found to be very little, if at all, deterred by the punishment inflicted upon other criminals, still many law-abiding citizens are very probably thus deterred. Many a man of exemplary conduct probably would, under provocations such as occur all too frequently, rob or murder some of his business associates or some of his relatives, if he did not have paraded before his eyes by every newspaper the example of what happens to people who do that sort of thing.

Society, then, is acting rationally in punishing offenders. By doing this it is successfully defending itself. Life is more satisfactory for most of the citizens because of the operations of the established penal system. Criminals really should be punished by society for their crimes. In other words they are morally responsible to society. From the social point of view they are culpable and guilty. The fact that a crime is 100% caused by hereditary and environmental conditions is absolutely irrelevant to the criminal's guilt, culpability, and moral responsibility.

Also irrelevant to his moral responsibility is the fact that, from his own point of view, penalties imposed are often bad, and thus ought not to be exacted. Incarceration or execution usually decreases his total satisfaction. At times it would be better for a criminal if he could escape. But still from the social point of view he ought not to. Society is then morally obligated to do what is, to him, an evil, because society needs to do this in its own self-defense. Punishing criminals is usually much more satisfactory for society in the long run than letting them off.

VI—Volition and freedom necessary for moral responsibility

An enlightened society holds a man morally responsible only for those acts which he has performed voluntarily. A man is not to blame for an evil deed unless he performed it freely. At the time that he did it he must have been capable of voluntarily doing some alternative if he preferred. Unless his evil deed was willed by him, anybody who punished him for it would be foolish and irrational and therefore immoral.

If it was willed by him his will should have been different. He was either malicious or negligent. Either he deliberately did a wrong to someone, or else his voluntary act was insufficiently motivated by an intent to avoid injuring his victim. Either malice or negligence must be present in a misdeed if its perpetrator is properly to be blamed for it. And this is the law. In order to secure a conviction, a prosecuting attorney has got to prove that the defendant experienced one or the other of these two defective states of will. If someone has been killed in traffic by an auto, and if the driver was not negligent and did not mean to kill his victim, then he (the driver) has committed no crime. He can kill any number of people in traffic without suffering any legal penalty so long

188

as he can prove that he did not mean to do it and that he was not negligent. However he is likely to have trouble proving this at his first trial. And at each subsequent trial the difficulty would increase greatly.

There are two reasons why men should be punished for none but their voluntary misdeeds. The first of these is that, as we have noted, vengeance is abnormal and irrational when the evil was done involuntarily. Ordinary people will not feel any satisfaction in taking vengeance on a man who has done damage unintentionally and without negligence. The second reason is that punishment will not help to protect society unless the deed was voluntary. Punishment is supposed to correct evil wills and attitudes. It is supposed to make men stop acting maliciously or negligently. But if an act was involuntary it was not due to any evil will or attitude. It was not due to any will at all. Also the chief legal punishments, execution and incarceration, are supposed to protect society by taking men of ill will out of circulation permanently or for a period, and putting them where they cannot do much or any damage. But the fact that a man has done some harm involuntarily and without negligence is no indication that he is more likely than anyone else to do further harm. There is no need of taking him out of circulation. And it will not deter others much from intentional or negligent damage if society punishes all persons who have done harm, even those who did it without these two defects of will. Only primitive societies punish people for involuntary acts. They do it because they do not understand some of the basic principles of justice. The chief aim of punishment is to discourage malice and negligence. If there has been neither, punishment is uncalled for, and therefore the perpetrator is not morally responsible.

VII—*Responsibility partly dependent upon the causation of the will*

While the mere fact that the original voluntary misdeed was determined is utterly irrelevant to the individual's moral responsibility for it, still certain causal influences upon future voluntary misdeeds are not irrelevant. If punishment will cause a man's will and his attitude to be less defective later on, that is a factor in making it worth while for society to demand and to inflict the punishment; and this social demand, we have seen, is what makes him morally responsible. Deterrence consists in this causation or determinism of his future will. Thus determinism of the will, far from destroying moral responsibility, helps to create it. Of course, there would be some rationality in punishment apart from deterrence, and therefore there would be some responsibility without it. But there would be nowhere near as much as there is in fact. Men would be much less responsible, that is, they would be much less liable to proper punishment, if penalties inflicted had no deterring effects, that is, no determining effects for the better, upon their wills and desires.

However, determinism has no other bearing on moral responsibility. The fact that in addition to this causal influence, wills are completely determined by various hereditary and environmental causes, does not in any degree either increase or diminish anybody's moral responsibility.

VIII—*Moral responsibility and reason*

We should also note that organisms are morally responsible about in proportion to the degree of their rationality. The more rational an individual is the more responsible he will be for his voluntary misdeeds. This is due to the fact that reason makes punishment more effective in correcting defects in his will. Thus it is more worth while for society to punish him on account of his errors.

Human adults who are blessed with normal intelligence are morally responsible for most of the evil and most of the good that they do voluntarily. Young children are less responsible. But so far as punishments and rewards will tend to influence them for the better, they are morally responsible. Also insane people, morons and the higher non-human animals, are commonly responsible for very little of what they do. So far as punishments cannot influence the behavior of an organism it is folly for anyone to punish it on account of the harm which it may have done. Oysters are utterly irresponsible because utterly devoid of reason.

IX—*Moral responsibility to self*

A man holds himself responsible for his good and his bad deeds through his own conscience. His conscience rewards him for his good deeds by its approval. It punishes him for his evil deeds by its condemnation. His conscience is the voice of his major interests, that is, of his better self. If he has a 'bad' conscience, these interests are crying out in his soul in protest at something which he had done. Really they are not bad. They are upbraiding him because he has been bad. He has disobeyed them. His better self demands that he shall live a certain type of life which is calculated to be the most satisfactory in the long run. And since this soul or self is a synthetical unity which is integrated through time, it demands that he shall always have lived that type of life. Such a retrospective desire is permanently thwarted if the

191

individual knows that he has not always done so. The suffering involved in the frustration of this desire is the punishment his conscience inflicts upon him. This punishment tends to correct his will and to improve his future conduct, so far as he is rational. His better self thus holds him morally responsible for his voluntary misdeeds because doing so is worth its while. It has an interest in making him answer for them. It cannot repudiate this interest without giving up its temporal, that is, its spiritual, integrity, that is, without abandoning its ideal of a total life which shall be of a type that is most satisfactory to it. To give up this ideal would mean spiritual disintegration.

X—Moral responsibility for good deeds

We have spoken chiefly of man's moral responsibility for his evil deeds. He is equally responsible for his good ones, so far as he is rational and acts voluntarily. He is responsible to society for his virtues so far as it should, from its own points of view, reward him for them. It should do this so far as the rewards it confers will confirm him in his good works, and perhaps lead others to emulate him. Society is constantly rewarding a good man negatively by not interfering with his circulating about freely in the pursuit of business and pleasure. Also an individual living a good life normally receives in return the almost constant expression of approval, respect, admiration, and affection from his family and friends. Without this, life can seldom be enjoyed. Moreover, various institutions, economic, political, recreational, etc., sometimes give him positive expressions of approval in the form of lucrative and honorable offices, and mention at public meetings, which usually please him most profoundly. Occasionally the state confers a great honor upon a man in the form of a Congressional medal, or it gives a general a triumphal procession through a large city as a reward for victories in the foreign field.

Also, as we have noted, men are morally responsible to themselves for their voluntary good deeds, so far as they are rational, since their consciences will rightly reward them for these and thereby confirm them in the paths of virtue.

Chapter XV

Art and morals

I—The nature of fine art

FINE ART is one form of the satisfaction of desire in the imagination. Partly it is an imaginative embellishment of real things which help or hinder practical interests, and partly it is a temporary escape from these interests. Schopenhauer said that it is a temporary escape from will into a realm of will-less contemplation. This is an error. Rather it is, in large measure, a temporary escape from the desires and predicaments of practical life, from the necessity of adjusting to reality, and from the industrious endeavor to control the environment, into the realm of imagination. In the sphere of adjustment, industry, and practical control, man is doomed to failure at many points. In the imagination his will can have its way much more fully, subject to one serious limitation, namely, that its success is merely imaginary. Fine art does not bring peace and joy by cancelling or ignoring will and desire in any Schopenhauerian renunciation. Rather it gives serenity by satisfying desire, but not in the real life of adjustment and control.

Fine art, then, is very much like play and day dreams and some night dreams in that it satisfies desire in the imagination. It differs from them in that it always finds public expression and it is superior to them in its formal perfection. Neither day dreams nor night dreams are ordinarily reported publicly. And neither dreams nor play commonly possess a high degree of formal perfection. If play ever does attain anything like this perfection it becomes a fine art, as when small children sometimes play house and enact a plot which attains the level of dramatic art.

In the fine arts life sometimes attains, for brief intervals and usually over restricted areas of experience, that perfection which it craves, in moments of spiritual insight, for the whole of life. Art is perfect, which is an advantage, but it is unreal in the sense of being only imaginary. Practical life is imperfect, but it is real, which is an advantage. Each has its limitations and each has its unique claim to our esteem.

II—Some principles of aesthetics that are universally valid in ethics

One of the great contributions of Professor DeWitt H. Parker to ethical theory in this generation is the application to ethics or general value theory of certain principles[1] which have been either worked out in the first place, or else clarified, in the field of aesthetics (theory of beauty). He has commented on this himself as follows in his presidential address before the Western Division of the American Philosophical Association in Cincinnati, Ohio, in 1929: " I came to the study of value through aesthetics, and not, as I believe most men do nowadays, through ethics. And this has been, I should claim, somewhat to my advantage, for literature and art represent a larger and freer attitude toward life than morality, which is inevitably traditional and dogmatic. It has interested me to discover how far one can carry concepts and principles which hold in the sphere of art into the gen-

---

1—These are to be found chiefly in his *Human Values* (1931) Ch. 2, 4, 15; and in his *Analysis of Art* (1926) Ch. 2.

195

eral field of value. Here, of course, I am but a humble follower in the footsteps of Pythagoras, who first gave to the notion of harmony, derived from his studies in music, its generalized ethical meaning."[2] In this he is using value in general to mean what I mean, and what he often means, by morality. And by 'morality' here he obviously means the traditional views of it.

The two chief principles which he has carried over from aesthetics to the general theory of value and duty are those of individualism or the plurality of ultimately authoritative moral standards, and the principle of harmony as the basic formal rule in all man's higher goods.

III—The plurality of ultimate standards in fine arts and in morals

The principles of the plurality of ultimate standards has been called anarchy by Professor Lucius Garvin of Oberlin in a paper in the *Journal of Philosophy*[3] (Jan. 29, 1942. Vol. 39, No. 3, esp. pp. 62-63). And he acquiesces in anarchy in the fine arts where, supposedly, the issues are not so vital. But he objects to anarchy in morals.

The plurality of ultimate standards in the fine arts is obvious. It should be clear that a work of art is not beautiful unless people enjoy it. And if one man or a number of men do not enjoy it, it is not beautiful for them, no matter what the majority think and no matter what the connoisseurs and critics say. Moreover, if an eccentric artist, say a composer, produces some music that is in violation of accepted standards, he may experience richer aesthetic delights from his

---

2—*Phil Rev.*, Vol. 38, No. 4, July 1929, p. 303.
3—Read at a meeting of the American Philosophical Association at Poughkeepsie, N. Y., in Dec. 1941.

work than he can from music which has been composed in the traditional manner. And a few odd folk may do likewise, while the bulk of the people may find it nauseating. If he gets more satisfaction in the long run from what is obnoxious to other people, then he is right, aesthetically, from his own point of view, in producing his own music. And the majority of the musically inclined people are right, from their points of view, in clinging to the traditions which they love. Obviously ultimate standards are plural. Of course, sometimes the musical innovation has something which the majority can learn to love in time, and when they do, they will sometimes love it more than the old traditional forms. If so, they are not right in sticking to their traditions. The fullest satisfaction of their desires, some of which are now hidden from them, will then be attained by accepting and studying the apparent idiosyncrasies of the truly great innovator. Their long range point of view is in accord with his; and he is then right not only from his own point of view but also from theirs. They shortsightedly condemned him at first only because they had failed to elucidate the depths of their own musical consciousness.

This, of course, is the case of Richard Wagner. But it is not the case of all eccentric composers. Some are rightly condemned by the musical public, even though they are right from their own points of view. Their weird compositions are beautiful to them, and ugly to the concert audiences.

This is axiological individualism. But it is not anarchy, provided that the bulk of the people are not forced to listen too frequently to the fantastic sounds which they hate so profoundly. Anarchy is a defiance of proper and accepted standards which does injury to others, or the absence of any authoritative standards which could prevent such injury. If the composer is socially innocuous he may be allowed to enjoy his idiosyncrasies in peace, unassailed by the stern derogatory epithet of 'anarchy.'

And the same principle applies to the field of action and of morals. If a man really gets the deepest satisfaction by walking up and down on top of his own wooden fence in his own back yard from 9 A.M. until 12 noon every day, he is right, from his own point of view, in doing this; and it is not anarchy. Moreover, society will probably not interfere, unless it is afraid that his aberrations may lead to something that is really dangerous.

For real anarchy, we may turn to the case of the criminal, which we discussed in Chapters 4 and 5. While awaiting execution, he might find his own highest good in escaping from jail. If he did, we must admit that he would be right, from his own point of view, in escaping. But his escape would violate accepted standards and would also injure others. It would be illegal, and it would threaten the security of the bulk of the people. It would be anarchy.

The people must put an end to anarchy if they can. The authority of social standards must be maintained. Each citizen has a duty, from his own point of view, to destroy the criminal's freedom and good if he can. The rightness of the criminal, *from his own point of view*, is irrelevant to the citizen's duty, *from his point of view*. The citizen must not serve the highest good of hostile organisms.

The same principle applies in art. A composer is allowed to be as eccentric as he likes, so long as he does not injure others. But sometimes he does injure others. His music may be put on a program by an adventuresome and hopeful conductor, and the audience may suffer. If they suffer enough the work will be consigned to oblivion. This is the punishment which the composer must suffer for his aesthetic sins. And it is a very severe punishment to the average composer. Some artists say that they do not care about fame. But in almost all cases when they say this they speak inaccurately.

Of course, there may be a composer or two who does not mind when people refuse to listen to his music; then the refusal of the public to listen is no punishment to him. He can still enjoy his work, and it is still most satisfactory, and therefore beautiful and right, to him. But the same holds, in the world of morals and action. If the criminal does not mind incarceration and execution, and perhaps torture or attempted torture, these are no punishment to him. If these should satisfy him most deeply in the long run they would be right from his point of view as well as from the social points of view. What effectiveness the penal systems have in civilized countries is due largely to the fact that the bulk of the criminals do not enjoy incarceration or execution or torture. No institution can be made to run without punishments. Human nature is not that perfect. And punishments are by definition things that people do not like.

By way of summary, then, the principle of the plurality of ultimate standards is valid both in ethics and in aesthetics. You are allowed to do or to compose anything you like unless it menaces or injures or bores or nauseates others. Whatever you do is right or beautiful, from your point of view, provided it satisfies you most fully in the long run. If it injures others they should, from their points of view, suppress your obnoxious activities.

IV—The formal principles of art and morals

The second basic principle which Professor Parker has

taken from aesthetics, and applied universally in ethics and in the general field of value, is the formal principle of harmony.[4] In Chapters 6 and 7 we referred to a ninth major interest in harmony. After having had a bit of experience, all rational people come to demand a certain amount of harmoniousness in their own lives and in the people about them and in society in general. Harmony is good because it satisfies, both in art and in morals. The highest good and the highest beauty can never be approached without it. Man's highest good requires that both the form and the content of life shall be right. The form is harmony. The content is chiefly the experience of the other eight major interests.

Synonyms for harmony are organic unity, unity in variety, and identity in difference. I think that 'harmony' and 'unity in variety' are the best expressions to use. Harmony is a union of two things, unity and variety.

There are three kinds of unity:

(1) There is the unity of a single particular element in art or in practical life, like a single patch of color in a painting, one note in a symphony, the mass of a single building as distinguished from two separate buildings, a word of praise, or an act of self-defense.

(2) There is the unity of similarity. So far as things are similar they all belong to one *class* or *category* or *kind*. A Greek temple has many similar columns, all belonging to one class of column. One element is said to be repeated again and again. In a Gothic cathedral the pointed arch and flying buttress are repeated many times. One kind of form appears again and again and gives to the building the unity of a single class of similar objects. In practical life an individual

---

4—See especially Parker's *Analysis of Art*, Ch. 2, and *Human Values*, Ch. 4.

of stable character does similar things year after year. His life is unified partly by this fact.

(3) A third kind of unity is collective unity. Any group of things related in any way, and perhaps given one name, makes a collective whole or unity. All of the heterogeneous buildings of a city or of one college campus are a collective unity. So are all of the heterogeneous people of any organized group. And so are all the divergent interests which make up one personality.

Variety obviously has three meanings also, each the opposite of one of the meanings of unity. Variety means several elements, it means dissimilar elements, and it means elements which are unrelated or whose relations are either unknown or ignored.

The advantage of unity is that it makes things simpler and easier to understand and to appreciate. It is restful. One element is easier to grasp than two. Two similar ones are easier to grasp than two different ones. The principle used for understanding the first can be used for the second. And elements somehow related in a collective whole are easier to comprehend than elements whose relations, if any, are unknown or ignored. Any understood relationship helps to hold the related terms or elements before the mind and to throw some light upon them.

The disadvantage of unity is that it tends to be too simple. It can be monotonous and boring. Variety is the spice of life. When we have enjoyed one thing for a while, let us turn to something else. To do so will probably be more fun.

Both fine art and all the rest of life need unity in order not to be disorderly and distracting and replete with frustrations. And both need variety in order to be interesting. Both need both unity and variety in order to be satisfying and beautiful and good.

V—The six subordinate formal principles

Under the main heading of harmony or unity in variety, there are six subordinate principles, each expressing some aspect or some application of the supreme principle. These are:

(1) Thematic repetition
(2) Thematic variation
(3) Contrast and Polarity
(4) Symmetrical balance
(5) Evolution
(6) Hierarchy, Dominance, Proportion, Non-symmetrical balance, the Golden Mean.

(1) *The repetition of a theme vs. uniqueness*

Every element in life and in fine art may be considered as a theme which is either to be repeated or else is unique and is not to be repeated.

A few themes are unique. Either they cannot be repeated or else they need not be. The classic example of any art form by its greatest master is unique. The Hermes of Praxiteles or Beethoven's third symphony are examples. Also first love and the birth of one's first child cannot happen again to anyone. And certain superlative triumphs need not be repeated. Mr. Churchill need not be called upon again to head England in her blackest hour, as he was called upon in May 1940. One call like that is enough for any man. He was prepared for it; he savored it fully in the consumma-

tion and in the retrospection, if not in the anticipation. Also
General MacArthur does not need again to enter Japan in
triumph.

But repetition of a theme is the rule, and uniqueness is
the exception. Men usually demand the repetition of any
enjoyable experience. This is partly because they are ever
ready to do something interesting, and they know that this
kind of an experience is so. Also, doing something once often
fails to exhaust its possibilities. One can savor it fully only
with many repetitions. In the first experience of anything,
one may have failed to pay proper attention to every aspect
of it.

In most musical compositions, several melodies and har-
monies are repeated again and again. In poetry the rime is
the repetition of a sound, and meter is the repetition of certain combinations of accented and unaccented beats. In a
painting colors and shapes are repeated in various parts of
the canvas. In a novel the permanent character of the hero
is shown repeatedly in his actions. In architecture a type of
arch or column or window or other element is repeated
many times in one building.

The major interests are the basic themes of all human
life inside and outside of the field of fine art, and thus, very
significantly, they are the basic themes of the practical life
of adjustment to reality and of the control of the environment. In ambition a man repeats the characteristic activities of his employment year after year, in order to maintain
and augment his position of power and influence in his community. A builder builds house after house. A teacher repeats his courses and his jokes year after year. In love and
friendship an individual repeats his expressions of affection for his beloved or his friend. In self-preservation he re-

peatedly takes precautions to guard himself from infection, from violent death in traffic, from starvation, and from other forms of quick or slow annihilation. In play, a family picnics in a pleasant spot of a Saturday afternoon, and they want to come back the next Saturday to do it again.

(2) *Variations on a theme.*

But mere repetition gets monotonous. A man wants to do most things once again, but not quite in the same way. Once he has savored an experience to the utmost he would like to vary the theme a little in order to get a new thrill. That is the way a man is built. Experience is more satisfactory that way.

In music, a phrase or melody may be repeated in another key or in another tempo or by another kind of instrument in the orchestra; or it may be shifted from the major into the minor. In poetry, the rimes repeat certain sounds but the words are different; the preceding sounds are different. And for the most part new riming sounds are used continually. Moreover, the feet of the meter are repeated, but with different words. In painting, a color is repeated at another place on the canvas, but perhaps with a slightly different shade or hue. And a shape is repeated at a different angle or in a different size. In a novel, the character of the hero expresses itself in different kinds of acts, and sometimes it develops new aspects without losing its basic continuity. In architecture, arches in a Gothic cathedral may be repeated in varying sizes in varying kinds of material (wood or stone, etc.) And gables or windows or chimneys may be varied in size while they retain certain basic similarities.

In practical life ambition finds expression through repetitions of the characteristic activities of the job. But there are variations. The builder puts new features into his later buildings. And the professor puts new facts, principles, and jokes into his courses as the years roll by. Love is a repetitious theme, but those friends and lovers are best who are always coming up with new interests and who always have something new to say. In self-preservation we sometimes benefit from new and improved methods of fighting off infection and sudden death. And in play, the family may picnic again in the same spot, but play different games and sing different songs, and have a different menu for the picnic lunch.

(3) *Contrast and Polarity.*

When things are different they tend to accentuate each other's values by contrast. Their oppositeness helps us to enjoy them. Also opposites sometimes produce a demand for each other. This is polarity. Repose creates a demand for exertion and exertion creates a demand for repose. And each is enjoyed more by contrast with the other. Staying home creates a demand for travel, and travel makes one long for home, and each enhances the value of the other. Love and home may fortify a man for the battles of his business life, and those battles may make him long for the relaxation of love and home. And again, contrast accentuates the value of each.

In music, the strings contrast with the brasses and a great deal of either one creates a demand for the other. Also fast and slow tempo are significant opposites; also loud vs. soft, and serenity vs. excitement. In fact, all of the contrasts of practical life are expressed abstractly in music. In poetry, the accented beats of the rhythm contrast with the unaccented beats.

205

In painting, light contrasts with shadow, blue with gold, and lines at right angles to each other emphasize the contrasts of direction and of motion. In a novel, the character of the hero and that of the villain are in contrast. Each accentuates the characteristics of the other. And in architecture the upward push of the vertical lines is in contrast with the downward push of the horizontal lines.

Rhythm, let us note here somewhat parenthetically, is not a distinct formal principle. It is a combination of repetition of a theme (the foot is the theme) with the contrast of the accented and unaccented beats. It is found not only in the temporal arts of poetry and music, but also in architecture, where one experiences it in moving one's eye along a row of columns or of flying buttresses. It is also present in some paintings where elements appear and disappear rhythmically as one's attention moves across the canvas or follows naturally certain lines that appear more prominently than others.

(4) *Symmetrical Balance.*

This means the equality or other similarity in some aspect of contrasting opposites. Opposites should not be utterly opposite, but should have some resemblances. In music, each bar has the same length, though somewhat different notes may appear in each. In poetry often every line, or perhaps every other line, has the same length. In painting, things of about equal interest should balance each other on either side of a central vertical axis, a horizontal axis usually a little below the center, and the two diagonal axes joining opposite corners. Some paintings are circular, and here segments (pie shaped sections) on opposite sides of the center should all balance. This is called radial symmetry. In architecture the wings of a building going in opposite directions from a central dome or tower or spire or gable, should usually be equal in bulk and should be made of the same kind of material. A big wing on one side and a little one on the other would be unbalanced. A red brick on one side and grey stone on the other would usually be terrible.

Symmetrical balance is less applicable in practical life than any other formal principle. Here contrasting elements almost never need to be equal. But they always need to be somewhat similar. When contrasts are established between love and ambition, exertion and relaxation, and travel and the comforts of home, all of these elements are similar in that they are the satisfactory experiences of one unified self, and that they function so as to accentuate the value of their opposites, and not to interfere with these seriously. But usually they need not be similar in any other way.

(5) *Evolution*

This means that some goal or purpose is attained step by step, and is clearly a case of unity in variety. The variety of steps is unified by their all serving the one end. The end, in a work of prose literature or of poetry, may be the clarification of an idea or the vindication of a moral principle. In a novel it may be the understanding of some person's character. Or the purpose may be to reveal a typical social situation, or to indicate the consequences of crime.

Sometimes the various steps lead to a sudden dramatic climax. Sometimes the purpose is attained bit by bit all along the way.

It is essential that the connection of each step with what has gone before and with what is coming after shall not be too difficult to grasp. If it is, the individual loses the sense of continuity, and usually loses interest and does not enjoy himself very much. Also the connection of each step with what has gone before and with what is coming after, must not be too obvious. If it is, the individual is bored and misses the element of excitement, and the surprise, which adds so much to the value of art and of life.

Evolution is exemplified more in the temporal arts than in the static ones. In music a melody leads the hearer along as it gradually reveals its total auditory pattern and its emotional meaning. Musical harmony is a series of cadences each of which is a sequence of chords leading the hearer through various transitorial stages to a solution. In most good novels, as in life, a man's character is revealed by a series of acts until in the end it stands out clearly before the mind of the reader. Or the consequences of some act are revealed step by step, as in the case of Macbeth.

The static arts sometimes exemplify evolution. In the side view of some great cathedrals, as one's eye travels from the back to the front, it gradually rises to the proud triumphant heights of the spire above the facade. Or in looking up a spire the eye is led step by step to an aesthetic and spiritual culmination at the pinnacle. The same applies when one looks up at a great dome from the inside. In a painting, attention may be carried across the canvas from a point of origin to a point of fulfillment, in an evolutionary progress. There may be many culminations, and some may be of a minor nature leading up to a major one.

In life, as in novels that portray it truly, a man's ambition is achieved step by step. If the steps are too hard he loses heart. If they are too easy, he is bored. If they are just hard enough to challenge him but not hard enough to stop him, he enjoys his onward progression. And the whole career is unified by some basic idea or purpose which stands out clearly to himself and to his friends, at least toward the end of the journey. Every step should contribute something, and no essential element should be omitted. Nothing should be irrelevant. Nothing should prevent the fulfillment of the basic purpose.

The same applies to a romantic love affair. It too must have an evolutionary unity in order to be deeply satisfying. And the same applies to the process of creating a work of art or the prosecution of research in science.

(6) *Hierarchy, Dominance, Proportion, Non-symmetrical Balance, the Golden Mean.*

This formal principle in some measure sums up all of the others. It means that in an organic unity, a human personality or a society or a work of fine art, there is a place for every element, and every element should be kept in its place. Things have varying degrees of importance, and they must not be allowed to occupy a position which is out of proportion to their true import. There are limits or boundaries to everything. Nothing must be allowed to overstep the bounds. Every element must receive its due emphasis, but none must be over-emphasized. Too much or too little of any impulse is bad. The Golden Mean is perfection. The elements of dominating importance must be allowed to dominate. And elements lower down in the hierarchy of importance and of value must be left in positions of subordination.

The violation of this principle produces an unbalanced life or an unbalanced society or an unbalanced work of art. But the balance here intended is not symmetrical balance.

Its violation does not mean that opposites have somehow become too unequal. To keep things of varying dignity and importance in balance is to keep them unequal. Equality here would be unbalance.

In music each theme must receive just enough reiteration and elaboration. If it is too long or not long enough, the composition is unbalanced. If it is too loud or not loud enough, also there is unbalance. In painting, especially, and in the novel, and in architecture, many examples will come to mind where an element can be over-emphasized or under-emphasized, and when perfection is the golden mean between these two.

In practical life it is the same. Each major interest is an element in the total personality interest. Each must be given its place and each must be kept in its place. There is a time to love and a time to defend oneself. There is a time to work for advancement, and a time to play, and a time to rest in comfort. And within each major interest the subordinate interests must function, each within the bounds set by reason and the plan of life and the formal requirements of harmony. Unity of purpose must be maintained, and yet there must be sufficient variety.

VI—*Life as an art*

To do all this is to make a well-balanced life. It is to fulfill the requirements of every formal principle. It is to raise life to its highest level and to live it at its best. To do this is the whole duty of man. To do this is to make of life an art.

Fine art means the satisfaction of desire in the imagination in accordance with the formal principles of harmony. *Art* may be used to mean the satisfaction of any desire, imaginative or practical, in accordance with these principles. To make life an art is to make it perfect. For this, both the form must be right and the content must be right. The form is harmony. The content is chiefly the satisfaction of the other eight major interests.

No one does this perfectly. But we can approach it with varying degrees of success. Fine art gives us a view of our goal usually in certain limited areas of our experience. It reveals to us for the most part limited and partial perfections that are beyond our powers of actual attainment. But some Gothic cathedrals and some Beethoven symphonies can express imaginatively and symbolically almost the whole of life.

VII—Art and Religion

One of the functions of religion is similar to that of fine art. It is to make vivid in men's minds the complete ideal of ultimate and total perfection, and to inspire people to approximate to this ideal as closely as possible. The love of God is an active devotion to this ideal. Whenever works of art succeed in expressing something near the whole of man's highest good they are truly religious in nature.

Religion uses social rituals, either church services and prayer or the performance of sacrifices at an altar, in order to vivify men's awareness of the ideal. In the more primitive types of religion, sacrifices, which may be the killing of a goat or the burning of incense, symbolize the devotee's dedication to the ideals for which the deity in question stands. In the literary form of religion, with sacred writings or a Bible, the group gathers and reminds itself of its ideals in songs and in prayers and in sermons which are based in some measure on the holy books.

In fine art, the ideal is symbolized mostly in physical objects, works of art, rather than in rituals. A work of art is something that an individual can pause and inspect when he has the time. However, symphony concerts approximate to the ritualistic symbolization of the ideal.

The importance of vivifying the ideal of man's highest good, and of inspiring people to devote their lives to it, can hardly be over-estimated. While final perfection is something that cannot be achieved in practice, still it is of utmost significance as the ultimate standard by which actual achievement should be appraised. It is one of the things that rational men have always included in their concept of God, and it is the religiously essential element in that concept. Man's vision of it is his ultimate guiding star and the criterion which he uses in constructing his idea of himself and his plan of life. This vision is the aspect of his self which tells the rest of his self what it ought to be and what it ought to do.

CHAPTER XVI

Humanistic Theism

I THINK that it is worth-while to formulate the essentials of religion in terms of a naturalistic philosophy.
I propose to call my formulation Basic Religion.[1] A rational interpretation of scientific discoveries, of history, and of ordinary experience, indicates that naturalism is true. Naturalism means two things. (1) It is a denial that there is any important purpose, apart from human purposes, running through the course of world events. It rejects cosmic teleology. (2) It means that every event is caused in strict accordance with uniform natural law. There are no uncaused events or miracles. The alleged supernatural is fictitious.

Contrary to much popular belief, the true essence of religion does not involve the supernatural. Religion can operate unimpaired with a naturalistic theology or metaphysics, provided that people understand the essentials.

Moreover, the preservation of civilization depends upon religion. Teaching the essentials is imperative. Religion can be taught in churches, homes, schools, or other institutions and places. Churches are especially designed for it. We had better use them as much as possible. We should seek to remedy their defects rather than find substitutes for them.

---

[1] I borrow this phrase from Professor Read Bain's article in the *Humanist*, for August 1950. His meaning is somewhat similar to mine, but he is not to be held for what I say.

The great need of a naturalistic Basic Religion flows from the two facts that naturalism is true and that religion is indispensable to man.

In Basic Religion there is a sort of Trinity of three important elements,—the supreme being, God, and the church. I shall try to define the first two very carefully, and to describe the essential functions of the third.

(1) The supreme being is the ultimate reality or substance of the universe. Modern physics indicates that it is structured energy, and that it is intrinsically non-teleological. It is the collective whole of all independent being, upon which everything else in the universe depends for existence. It is what has been called God the Father, the Creator of all dependent being such as consciousness or experience. But I think that it should not be called God. It does everything, including all the evil. Whatever does evil, is, to that extent, evil. It is not a proper object of religious devotion. It is omnipotent in the sense that it has the power to do everything which is actually done, not that it could do anything at all. It could not make two plus three equal six without adding another one either openly or surreptitiously. But we owe all of our blessings to it, and if we are so inclined we may well feel a pious gratitude to it for them. This cosmic piety to the supreme being is one aspect of religion. However, it is not indispensable. No one need express it who does not feel like doing so.

Calling the ultimate substance a 'being' merely means that it exists, and does not necessarily mean that it is a person or a living being. But part of the supreme being is present in every human being. A man is, substantially, a constellation or integration of some of the structured energy of the universe. He is caused to be what, at any moment, he is, partly by the past natural processes that have gone on in that constellation, and partly by the environmental influences of other structures of energy. All of the conscious life of man, including such spiritual factors as a passion for truth or a love of justice, are emergent properties of the integrated functioning of the energies that make up his organism, chiefly those constituting his nervous system.

The supreme being is a collective whole of all the structured energy there is.

(2) This being should be sharply distinguished from God, who or which is the abstract principle of divinity and duty. God is the ideal, standard, or principle of man's highest good. Many responsible theologians, including St. Thomas, have endorsed this view of deity. Man's highest good is that which would be most deeply satisfactory to man in the long run. We have seen that in one sense it is purely individual and in another universal. It is that to which man can give, rationally, the last full measure of devotion. It is the object of his chronically recurrent rational drive toward perfection.

The spiritual validity of this principle of divinity harmonizes perfectly with a naturalistic metaphysics. It is not a natural force. It determines logically and absolutely what is right and wrong. Many have inferred from these facts that it must be a supernatural force. But it is no force at all. The worship of force is a most deplorable element in nearly all traditional organized religion. The standard of man's highest good is an abstract principle, like two plus three equals five. It is eternal in two senses. It is changeless, and time is irrelevant to its operation. Any supposed alteration just makes another principle, such as that two plus two-and-nine-tenths make five, or that 'to suffer in the flesh is man's greatest glory.' These false principles are eternally invalid. The true ones are eternally and changelessly valid. Time is irrelevant to their operation in two senses. Nothing that happens or fails to happen in time can invalidate them, and it does not take time for them to function. The first is obvious. As to the second, clearly it does not take time for two plus three to make five, nor for the principle of man's highest good to make an act right which conforms to it.

The essential thing in religion is an active devotion to this principle, ideal, or standard. Such devotion is the love of God. Man's duty to God comes first. It ought to take precedence over everything else in life. Thus Basic Religion is theistic. It is Humanistic Theism.

The meanings of God and the supreme being which I employ here are generally used, but all of my readers will be aware that other meanings are also used. When a definition is called for, these other meanings are the ones which people almost invariably offer. Indeed, these are usually insisted upon as the only proper meanings. Both the currency and the propriety of my meanings are often denied.

It is not unusual for people to use a term in one sense and, when challenged to explain their meaning, give a definition with complete sincerity which formulates a different sense of the term. It may be very difficult for one to say clearly exactly what he means, especially in a field where popular feeling is so intense and so primitive, and where the very existence of certain churches seems to depend upon the confusion of thought.

I believe that my meanings are in many cases the ones which people actually use, and that they are the ones which people ought always to use. With these meanings, and in the light of science and of a true naturalistic philosophy, religion can be properly understood, candidly expressed, socially accepted, and sincerely practiced in the present age.

However, the true essence of basic religion is contained in all prevalent religions. This essence is, to repeat, an active devotion to the ideal of man's highest good. It is the love of God. I did not invent my definitions. I found them in the religious tradition of Western Civilization. They are used in religious life to-day along with others which in some cases contradict them. I adopted them because they seemed to me to be good, true, and current. I believe that it is because these definitions are used and acted on in all religion that civilization depends for its existence upon religion.

(3) In the absence of supernatural help, the function of the church is to give social corroboration to man's higher aims, admonition as to his lower ones, and general guidance in the conduct of his life. The supreme being functions as God the Father in the sense of a creator. The church functions as God the Father in the sense of a loving spiritual-social protector, guide, philosopher, and friend. Man needs its ministrations in order that he may live as nearly as possible according to the divine (logical and natural) principle of his highest good.

Those who incline to a narrow theological traditionalism often hold that the church is primarily a channel through which supernatural grace and power are conveyed to man, and that it is this grace and power which really corroborate, admonish, and guide. Such a view is often associated with the notion that human life would be meaningless, futile, and worthless if it were not the working out of a divine cosmic purpose. Many believe that their own highest aspirations are particular forms taken by a cosmic power, will, or intelligence, a portion or aspect of which is present in their lives.

217

If this were so their higher aspirations would be intrinsically corroborated by the cosmic will, and their lower ones intrinsically admonished. The belief that this is so gives them a great deal of self-confidence in trying to realize their higher aspirations. The good side of traditional religion consists largely in the fact that it gives this self-confidence to many people. One bad thing about most traditional religion is that it misleads people as to the facts. The cosmic power or purpose, to which it appeals, probably does not exist. Those who have, through a rational interpretation of scientific knowledge, understood the truth of evolutionary naturalism, will realize that there is not much evidence for any cosmic purposive power. People believe in it because they wish that it existed, because of the tradition about it created chiefly by men's wishes in an unscientific and an unenlightened age, and because of social teaching and pressure that make many feel morally culpable when they disbelieve in it.

The prevalence of this wish-thinking and social pressure make some people suspect that all religion would be ruled out if naturalism is true. But if religion is essentially the three things I have said it is, the supreme being, God, and the church, it is not ruled out by naturalism.

People who have been nourished on illusion sometimes do in fact feel that if their belief in cosmic corroboration were destroyed, life, for them, would become meaningless, futile, and worthless. Many are spiritually crushed when their own intelligent interpretations of scientific truths gradually reveal to them the groundlessness and the falsehood of this belief. Some commit suicide. But these tragedies do not indicate the truth of that belief, the loss of which caused the tragedies.

Man needs corroboration in his highest aspirations. He

gets it from other people. Churches are organized to give it to him. Most churches now can do a better job with the bulk of their clients by claiming to be channels of supernatural or cosmic corroboration, admonition, and guidance. At a low level of culture people will not respect anything unless it is thought to be supernatural. They will prize what is really noble, that is, what is deeply satisfying in the long run, only if it is presented to them as being sponsored by a supernatural force. That which is spiritually great must be thought to have a transcendent meaning and value, because its purely human intrinsic value cannot be grasped at that level of culture.

When people are helped, as they so frequently are, by this sort of mythical ideology, the actual process which the church carries on is purely one of social corroboration, admonition, and guidance. The supernatural claim, accepted by the devotee, simply makes the social institution seem more authoritative. This claim makes it a more effective human corroborator, admonisher, and guide.

Enlightened people sometimes become antagonistic to the church when they discover that its supernaturalism and cosmic teleology are false. But they should realize that by means of its mythical supernaturalism it is performing an indispensable social function in a manner comfortable to religious life at a low cultural and intellectual level. Many people who are enlightened in other areas of human experience may be quite primitive on the religious side.

The tremendous importance of social corroboration, admonition, and guidance should be recognized. No man can trust himself unless some of those whom he respects trust him. He cannot believe that he is doing what is right unless they indicate to him that they think he is doing so. He cannot believe what the evidence of his experience, interpreted by reason, overwhelmingly indicates to be true, unless they agree.

But social corroboration is always imperfect. Those who corroborate us are somewhat selfish and unreliable, like ourselves. Moreover, they need our corroboration, admonition, and guidance, just as much as we need theirs. The imperfections in all the social corroboration we get have led men to imagine a perfect cosmic corroborator, admonisher, and guide. But a more sensible cure for these imperfections is to try to improve the corroboration on the human and social level. This is the task of the church. Churches should study how to perform their essential function more effectively in a changing culture that is gradually becoming less primitive in its religious thinking. Ministers should be trained more in psychiatry and less in Greek. This work can be done now, for more and more people, intelligently, scientifically, naturally, humanly, and lovingly, without mythology or supernaturalism. The church can try to foster intellectual enlightenment, and the rational interpretation of science, instead of combatting these things, as it now does so frequently.

INDEX

Ambition (will-to-power), 3, 6, 63-64, 78-80, 90, 100
Anarchy, 196-198
Anderson, B. M., 142n
Anthropology, 15-16
Anticipatory interests, 2, 105-106, 110-114
Aristotle, 11-13, 37, 49, 60, 76, 162
Art, 13-14, 57, 87, 100, 194-212
Augustine, St., 128
Axiological absolute, 23, 27-28; see Primary value, Feeling of satisfaction

Bain, R., 213n
Barnes, Hazel E., 102n
Basic religion, 213, 216
Battles of the gods, 45, 48
Bentham, J., 133-134
Bergson, H., 140-147
Biological evolution, 14-16, 59, 74, 100, 122, 165, 178, 181
Butler, J., 91

Calvin, J., 30
Categorical imperative (right, duty), 1, 10, 28-30, 36, 39, 44-46, 54-55, 136, 200, 215-216
Causation, 116-120, 152-155, 165-173, 176-177; Container theory of causation, 15, 118, 122, 166-170; see Determinism
Chance, 173-174
China, 62
Choice, 17, 30-31, 95-96, 142-146, 148, 154-158
Christian love, 34, 69, 71, 133
Churches, Function of, 213, 217-220
Cognitive indeterminism vs. causal indeterminism, 153-154
Communication, 25
Comte, A., 18
Conscience, 106-107, 111, 191-192
Consummatory interests, 2, 109-110, 114
Contrast, 202, 205-206

Cosmic teleology, 1, 8, 12, 213, 217-219
Criminals, 42, 44, 46-47, 51-52, 75, 139-140, 175, 186-189, 199
Cultural evolution, 15-16, 122, 165
Cultural relativity of value, 17

Death, 90-91, 130
Descartes, 20
Desire, 54; see Major interests
Determinism, 14, 17, 149-193
Dialectic, 19-22, 46
Duty; see Categorical imperative

Eddington, A. S., 14, 151-153
Efficiency, 88
Emergence, 1, 15, 17, 94, 122-123, 135, 165, 178
Empirical rationalism, 18; see Rationalism
Epicurus, 4, 13, 28, 37, 60, 121-132, 151
Evolution, 1, 15, 122, 165; Evolution as an art-form, 202, 207-209; see Biological evolution, Cultural evolution, Naturalism
Extrinsic good; see Instrumental good

Family life, 65-69
Fatalism, 179
Feeling of satisfaction, 4, 17, 22-23, 54-55, 82-83, 123, 132, 140-147; see Axiological absolute, Primary value
Formal principles of art and morals, 199-210
Free-will, 1, 17, 148-193
Freud, S., 17, 62
Fromm, E., 18, 132

Garvin, L., 196
God, 11-12, 18, 45, 49-50, 132, 211-212, 214-220
Golden mean, 202, 209-210
Goldsmith, O., 74
Group mind, 25
Guilt (remorse), 96, 191-192

221